MOLTKE'S CORRESPONDENCE

DURING THE

CAMPAIGN OF 1866 AGAINST AUSTRIA.

PRÉCIS

BY

SPENSER WILKINSON,
*Chichele Professor of Military History,
Fellow of All Souls' College, Oxford.*

WITH FOUR PLANS.

The Naval & Military Press Ltd

Published and © by the
The Naval & Military Press

In reprinting in facsimile from the original, any imperfections are inevitably reproduced and the quality may fall short of modern type and cartographic standards.

PREFACE.

BETWEEN 1892 and 1902 the historical department of the Prussian Great General Staff published six volumes of Moltke's Military Correspondence, one of which entitled "From the Official Papers of the War of 1866," appeared in 1896. It contains 364 documents with the briefest possible connecting and explanatory text. The documents are arranged in four parts, the first entitled "Preparations for the War," the second "Mobilization and Deployment," the third "The Actual War," in two sections, of which the first is concerned with the campaign against Austria and Saxony, and the second with the campaign in Western Germany. The fourth part is entitled "Armistice and Peace."

In 1896, by way of preparation for an essay on Moltke's projects for the campaign of 1866 against Austria, which appeared in the "United Service Magazine" of July in that year, I made a précis of the documents contained in the first part of the German volume, omitting those which concerned the operations against Hanover, Hesse and the South German States. In 1902, at the suggestion of the then Director-General of Military Intelligence, Sir William, now Lord Nicholson, this précis was printed by his department and has since been published by the General Staff.

As the campaign against Austria is one of those studied for the Honours School of Modern History at Oxford I have now carried on the précis to the end of Part III, Section 2, that is to the Armistice of Nickolsburg which terminated the campaign against Austria. The campaign in Western Germany and the period of the armistice have not been included. The Imperial General Staff, which has heartily co-operated with the University in all that concerns the study of Military History, has kindly undertaken to publish this continuation of the précis, which, in conjunction with the volume already published, gives a complete account of Moltke's work in the preparation for and conduct of the principal part of the great central campaign of the nineteenth century.

The attempt has been made to reproduce in full and as nearly as may be in Moltke's own words the more important of the papers and to compress the others into the smallest space compatible with a grasp of the subject. Occasionally merely the number and title of a document are given. In this way the reader will always know when anything is withheld from him and can, if he wishes, refer either to the original or to the excellent French translation. Army Corps are described by Roman numerals and the Guard Corps by the letter G. The explanatory and connecting text is given in brackets. This précis is published by permission of Messrs. E. S. Mittler and Sohn of Berlin. Two of Moltke's letters not contained in the Prussian collection are translated from the second edition of "Lettow-Vorbeck's" excellent history of the war and are here published also by the kind permission of Messrs. E. S. Mittler and Sohn of Berlin. An outline general map of Germany in 1866 accompanies the précis of Part I, entitled "Moltke's Projects for the Campaign of 1866 against Austria."

SPENSER WILKINSON.

May 7th, 1914.

PART II.

MOBILIZATION AND ASSEMBLY.

On May 3rd was ordered the mobilization of the cavalry and artillery of the line, and of the Guard III, IV, V and VI Army Corps; thereupon Moltke handed in the following proposal for posting the five mobile Army Corps:—

No. 53.

To the King.

Berlin, May 4th.

Yesterday Your Majesty graciously ordered the mobilization of the five army corps first threatened by the Austrian concentration, but reserved the determination of the places of assembly of these corps.

The positions in which they will first assemble directly affect any operations which may afterwards be necessary, and I therefore respectfully venture to submit to Your Majesty the following:—

There are stationed at present along the railway from Josephstadt to Olmütz and Brünn 21 Batn., 5 Cav., 2 Art. Regts.; from Tetschen to Prague 21 Batn., 4 Cav., 1 Art. Regt.

Accordingly within three days there can be assembled 30,000 Austrians, either in the neighbourhood of Trautenau or at Tetschen or even at Dresden. Reports, which until now have not been definitely confirmed, speak of 12,000 men posted at Troppau and certainly a corps of this or greater strength could be assembled there in 14 days by bringing up the troops from Galicia, or sooner if the movement has already begun.

Thus upper and middle Silesia, Lusatia and the district of Torgau are the regions at present threatened.

From this point of view and with a view to later operations it seems suitable to assemble:—

VI Army Corps at Neisse, where it can be on the 17th day.
V Army Corps at Schweidnitz, where it can be on the 20th day.
III Army Corps at Cottbus, where it can be on the 22nd day.
IV Army Corps at Torgau and westwards, where it can be on the 22nd day.
Guard Corps, in the first at instance Berlin, where it can be on the 22nd day.

The corps cannot be at the points named on the dates given unless Your Majesty now authorizes the Central Railway Commission immediately to carry out the necessary preparations upon the lines concerned with their transport.

These preparations, necessary for any transport on a large scale, in this case as in that of the possible later mobilization of other corps, must take place during the first ten days, during which the corps are collecting their men and horses. Unless, therefore, their arrival at their points of assembly is to be delayed by as many days, the orders for the transport must be issued at the same time as those for mobilization. In moving to the positions here suggested a corps will march by road wherever and whenever that is possible without delaying the date of arrival of the whole. The time-tables for the trains and the marches are ready at the General Staff, awaiting Your Majesty's approval.

With regard to the concentration of VI at Neisse, I beg to point out that at this moment Breslau is most directly threatened along the line from Trautenau by Schweidnitz, as the first part of V, composed of all arms, does not reach Schweidnitz till the fourteenth day, and as this place in its partly demolished condition cannot be left to the enemy, and can very well be held for a few days against a coup de main, it might be advisable to leave at Schweidnitz, until that day, when they will be relieved, the 1st Silesian Grenadier Regiment No. 10 and the 4th six-pounder battery of the Silesian Field Artillery Regiment No. 6.

The assembly of VI at Neisse is to be taken only in the sense that the main body will there assemble. The detachments which are now at Glatz, Cosel and Ratibor, especially the 12th Cavalry Brigade, might even after mobilization remain to watch the border until the enemy actually crosses it, and all detailed arrangements for this purpose might be left to the general commanding VI, who must alone be responsible for the defence of this part of Silesia until the arrival of larger forces.

But the infantry of this corps will even then not be available until the Landwehr Battalions reach the fortresses of Glatz, Neisse and Cosel, which can be arranged by the sixteenth day if Your Majesty is pleased now to order their transport by railway in so far as the railway must be used; if they must all march they cannot arrive except between the twenty-fourth and thirty-first days.

(His Majesty discussed these proposals with the Minister of War, who afterwards informed the Chief of Staff that His Majesty had approved the proposals, with the modification that the III Army Corps and 7th Division should be placed between Cottbus and Torgau, to which district the cavalry of the 8th Division should march. Part of the infantry of the 8th Division was to remain at Erfurt until this fortress had received its normal garrison. Whether one brigade of III should be placed at some other point was reserved for further consideration. Of VIII, of which the King ordered the mobilization on May 5th, one brigade was to be posted at Wetzlar, while the rest of the troops of this corps were to assemble at Coblenz.)

No. 54.

To General Baron von Manteuffel.

Suggestions for the Seizure of Holstein.

Things now stand so that I hold war certain. A telegram of to-day reports continuous transports. For to-morrow two infantry regiments and a Rifle battalion due at Troppau. Italy will certainly strike her blow. There great enthusiasm, while with us corporations making demonstrations in favour of peace.

What has been decided in the highest quarters during the last few days I do not know, but believe that, if the safety of the State is not to be endangered, the mobilization of the army must not be postponed more than by hours.

No. 55.
To Roon.

Berlin, May 7th.

(Steinmetz, commanding V, had written to Roon that he proposed to assemble V between Liegnitz and Schweidnitz. Moltke writes to say that):

From the moment that arrangements are in progress for concentrating the army, generals commanding army corps must not interfere with the railway administration. Approves of the proposed assembly of V. Thinks that of VI may be left to its commanding general. But for IV, G and III, the boundaries which are to separate their cantonments must be given. Within the regions thus bounded the commanding generals may do as they please but the moment there is a prospect of hostilities must close up their corps, so that each corps can be concentrated in one day and all three in two more days.

No. 56.
To Roon.

May 7th.

Desirable to construct a few field works at Schweidnitz to delay the enemy in case of sudden attack.

No. 57.
*Memorandum.**

Berlin, May 7th.

It may shortly be all important to protect Berlin against an attack.

An advance can be made from the line Dresden—Bautzen either along the road—

      A. Herzberg—Luckenwalde,
  or B. Cottbus—Lübben,
  or C. between both.

* See plans 2 and 3.

Considering that the troops may perhaps be kept a long time in their cantonments we ought to give our corps an extension of 9 square miles (German miles. 1 German mile = $4\frac{1}{2}$ English miles = 7·5 kilometres).
Say—

    III. Cottbus, Calau, Spremberg, Senftenberg,
    IV. Torgau, Mühlberg, Elsterwerda, Dobrilugk, Herzberg,
    G. north of both at Luckau.

Advance guards on the Elster at Hoyerswerda (III) and Elsterwerda (IV).

Concentration of the corps each in itself at Drebkau, Liebenwerda, Finsterwalde requires one day; assembly of all three corps at Senftenberg four days; Elsterwerda three days; Luckau, Lübben three days. The question now is, assuming the enemy in superior force—

Where is it proposed in the one case or the other to accept a defensive battle?

(A.) Most probable case; the enemy advances by Elsterwerda.

(Position a.) Elsterwerda—Plessa.

One mile front, near the frontier, on the main road. Strong obstacle in front can be turned on the left flank only through Bockwitz and Ruhland—detour of two miles (15 kilometres = 9 English miles). Right flank protected by the Elster. But little depth, surrounded on all sides by forest, troops on the left wing almost superfluous because cannot be attacked, altogether position rather for a division than for three corps, no offensive to the front, enemy's approach hard to perceive. The assailant would have nothing left but to move into the ground between Elster and Elbe, in which case we meet him without difficulty on the line Elsterwerda-Liebenwerda with the Elster in our front.

If enemy advances further, in which case he must detach against Torgau, we can follow him on the right bank of the Elster and when he finally crosses at Jessen and Schweinitz we shall be on his flank. Accordingly if this position is to be occupied—

Advance Guard. One division Elsterwerda. (Cahla, Plessa only slightly held—reconnaissance from and above Mückenberg.)

Main body—Three divisions south of Hohenleipisch to give emphatic support to the front. (Prieschka, Würdenhain, Saathain on the left bank all occupied.) Cavalry corps in cover south of Kraupa.

Reserve.—Two divisions village of Weinberg. (Liebenwerda occupied.)

Detachment to keep touch at Stolzenhayn with retreat through Oschätzchen to Liebenwerda.

Possibility of offensive of main body across Elster if enemy follows that direction.

In case position is turned by Ruhland the retreat to Dobrilugk—Kirchhain is out of enemy's reach.

(Position b.) Moglenz—Burxdorf. 1 mile front. 1 division Elsterwerda. Strong battery at Burxdorf. Elbe and Hassenbusch secure the right flank; the Elster marshes the left flank.

Advance guard pushed forward to Stolzenhayn.

Retreat upon Torgau or upon Berlin.

Enemy's deployment extraordinarily embarrassed.

He cannot conveniently attack the position until he has dislodged the division which at Elsterwerda stands on the flank of his advance, accordingly will probably require two days.

Attack upon Elsterwerda can succeed only through Saathain—Heida, but in that case our advance guard must first be driven out of Stolzenhayn; to perform this task 40,000 to 50,000 men necessary. Our division from Elsterwerda falls back to Liebenwerda, advance guard to Cröbeln. An advance of the enemy's forces engaged before Elsterwerda or of his whole army on the right bank of the Elster not to be assumed (least of all an attempt to turn Liebenwerda by side roads) seeing that we, based on Torgau, can advance offensively on the rear of this movement and that Berlin is still five or six marches distant.

The advance of so large a part or the whole of his army along the left bank across the Great and Little Röder will meet with great difficulties in the nature of the ground and of the roads.

The advance of a portion through Göhrisch—Heide involves an objectionable separation of forces.

Therefore probably previous concentration, deployment Cosilenzien—Vw. Wendisch-Borschütz, attack on our right wing.

Detached.

One division (that from Elsterwerda) occupying Lausitz—Liebenwerda and Wahrenbrück (if the enemy does not advance on the right bank of the Elster this division can act against his right flank).

Main Body.

One division Möglenz—U.F.
One division Burxdorf Station to Burxdorf.

Reserve.

Two divisions between Haasenbusch and Grüne Heide behind Langenrieth. Cavalry concealed behind the corner of the wood of Haasenbusch.

Advance Guard.

One division at Cosilenzien withdraws to Grüne Heide.

The southern prolongation of the Grüne Heide is inconvenient for the defence but in compensation there is a good field of fire and a free offensive of both wings in case of attack on the centre.

As this position has been judged merely from the map nothing but an actual inspection of it can decide its *local* value, in particular the nature of the ground in front, the meadow of Ziegeram, importance of the courses of the Great and Little Röder.

(B) The operation through Cottbus and thence round the east side of the Spreewald is not to be expected; we should be beforehand with it at the defiles of the Spree.

The enemy may use the roads Spremberg, Cottbus—Vetschau and Senftenberg—Calau. To anticipate him between Senftenberg—Spremberg is hardly possible even if a strong advance guard be pushed forward to Hoyerswerda. Moreover, the ground between Senftenberg and Spremberg seems little suited for a decisive battle, and the same must be said of the wooded region of Lower Lusatia, which stretches behind it for several miles. But the union of the three corps can be effected with certainty at Luckau where the position Karche—Duben would have to be occupied against an enemy advancing from Vetschau and Calau. Front 1 mile. Left wing covered by the marshes of Terpt. Right by the Börste. Luckau in front of the right and flanking the attack to be occupied.

Strategic turning of left flank impossible because of the Spreewald: Cottbus—Lübben six miles (27 English miles) Duben—Lübben 1 mile (4½ English miles); to turn the right a flank march of 4 miles (18 English miles) past our front on forest roads Calau—Wüstermark would be required.

Retreat after lost battle impeded by Lower Börste which,

however, has several crossings between Lübben and Kasel. We could rally behind it and afterwards behind the Dahme.

No obstacle in front but freedom for the offensive; field fortification desirable.

Position.

Three divisions in first line; Luckau occupied by a brigade on the Schanzenberg (*i.e.*, hill N.W. of Luckau).

Three divisions in reserve.

(C) As the line of march through Cottbus makes a circuit very far eastward it is possible that the enemy would follow the road Kamenz—Senftenberg—Calau and Konigsbrück—Ruhland—Finsterwalde.

In that case we should take a position at Dobrilugk—Kirchhain, which seems to be very strong for defence and past which the enemy could not march upon Sonnenwalde. He would be compelled to bring up his column from Senftenberg to attack us. If he did not we should take the offensive, based on Torgau.

I consider it quite impossible for the enemy to march on Berlin—8 or 10 marches—without first attacking us if we stand with 100,000 men either at Burxdorf, Elsterwerda or Dobrilugk. I therefore attach little importance to a concentration at Luckau, the important thing being only so to place our three corps that we can have them ready in good time in one of the three positions first named.

It is therefore desirable as soon as possible to bring III further to the west.

If III stands at Senftenberg the enemy can hardly take the Cottbus road without first attacking us.

It has then only two marches to Dobrilugk or Elsterwerda or to the left wing of the Burxdorf position.

On May 26th the III Corps can be ready for action in one or other of these positions, provided the Guard Corps can march off from Berlin on 18th.

No. 58.

To the Minister of War.

Encloses a pamphlet giving an account of the Austrian army.

No. 59.
To Tresckow.

About the formation of staffs. Shows that Moltke hoped to get rid of army corps commanders and preferred to work by divisions.

No. 60.
To von Mutius.

Approves of Mutius' plans for posting VI. Railway details.

No. 61.
To Roon.

Urging completion of railway line as far as Cottbus.

No. 62.
To Stosch, Chief of Staff of IV.

Explains rayons in which III, IV and G are to be distributed and that in case of need the points of assembly would be—

    III. Döbern, or Senftenberg.
    G. Luckau, or Sonnenwalde.
    IV. Liebenwerda.

No. 63.

Dispositions of IV.

No. 64.
To Roon.

May 9th.

Austrian mobilization nearly ended, railway transport of Austrian army may begin at any moment.

No. 65.
To Roon.
Further details of Austrian preparations.

No. 66.
To Roon.

May 14th.

Austrian railway transport began on 11th. Benedek reached Vienna on 12th.

No. 67.
To Roon.

May 17th.

Reports indicate that Austrian principal forces are assembling between Pardubitz and Weisskirchen.

No. 68.
To Chief of Staff of VI.

May 12th.

Question where I is to be sent—to Görlitz or Breslau? Moltke prefers Breslau.

Incidentally discusses defensive on line Neisse—Frankenstein—Landeshut.

(By May 12th mobilization of whole army ordered. May 14th Moltke reported to King):—

No. 69.
Notes for Audience.

8th Federal Corps, nominally 40,000, said to be collecting in Würtemberg. It can hardly intend to operate independently against us but might join Bavarian 40,000 about Bamberg. These 80,000 will take a long time to get ready and be concentrated.

Meanwhile a much stronger army will soon be actually ready in Northern Bohemia and Saxony.

Saxons apparently intend to concentrate at Annaberg. Austrians in view of our force in Lusatia and Silesia can hardly spare an army corps to support the Saxons on the left bank of the Elbe. So Saxons probably mean to join Bavarians in Franconia.

Accordingly we have to dispose our forces to meet an enemy distributed on the line Bamberg—Prague. In our rear we have to watch the Hanoverians, who with the Brigade Kalik will make about 23,000 men.

If we tried to meet with an equal force these 100,000 Federal troops not yet ready we should have to face with inferior forces the Austrian army which will be quite ready. VIII at Coblenz, 13th Division at Minden, and 8th Division at Erfurt would probably stand waiting while the decisive battles were fought on the border of Bohemia.

In the position in which we are it seems more advisable to assemble all our forces against the principal enemy, the more so as a first victory over him will probably prevent our other opponents from acting at all. But in that case we must immediately employ a reinforced division to act against Hanover, and for this purpose it must be kept ready at Minden. The other three divisions of our Western Corps would at Coblenz be further from Bamberg than if they were assembled between Halle and Zeitz, where they would be ready to co-operate from the beginning either against the Saxons or against the Austrians.

If it should later on be necessary to proceed against Bavaria an offensive can, if these dispositions are made, be supported from the main army, as it could not be if the Rhenish troops had to start from Coblenz.

I therefore propose—

1. 13th Division reinforced to assemble at Minden. 6,000 men from Holstein could co-operate, which gives against Hanover 30,000 men, quite enough for the purpose.
2. VIII and 14th Division to be brought to Zeitz and Halle: 45,000 men can drive the Saxons either into Bavaria or into Bohemia, and if they go into Bohemia can follow them, if to Bavaria can observe them from Plauen.
3. 8th Division to 1st Army.
4. II to Herzberg, also 1st Army.

5. I to Görlitz.
6. Reserve Corps marches towards Saxony, ready to start on June 8th.

If Austrians, with main force, take the offensive against the 1st Army, they would probably have to leave weak forces facing Silesia in order to be superior to the 1st Army, so 2nd Army would at once take the offensive.

If the Austrian main force invades Silesia five divisions there would act on the defensive, while 1st Army would march into Bohemia.

In case it is not thought fit to denude the Rhine Province of troops I would propose to leave 16th Division at Coblenz, 13th Division at Minden, but to move 14th and 15th Divisions to Zeitz and 8th Division to Herzberg.

No. 70.

Same proposals in writing.

Effect of proposals will be by June 4th—

45,000 men against Saxony.
130,000 ,, in Lusatia.
34,000 ,, at Görlitz.
60,000 ,, in Silesia.

and by June 7—

24,000, reserve corps, at Frankfurt-on-Oder or Berlin.

No. 71.

To Roon.

May 21st.

On Brigade Kalik, Mainz and Hanover.

No. 72.

Draft Order for Governor of Mainz.

No. 73.
Notes for Audience of May 25th.

(*a*) Austrian offensive. At beginning of June Austrians may have 180,000 men, and if they leave 60,000 to face what we have in Silesia might start with 120,000 towards Berlin. In that case in six days we can have III, IV, II, G, and if necessary also either VIII or I about Elsterwerda, in any case five corps with 150,000 to 165,000 men.

Therefore no danger for Berlin.

(*b*) The Austrians might invade Silesia with more than 120,000 men if they throw over the Saxons. In that case 12th Division at Kosel protects Upper Silesia as well as it can—retreat by Oppeln and right bank of Oder.

Rest of the two corps (V and VI), 45,000 to 50,000, assemble at Landeshut to resist invasion from Trautenau. Retreat not to Breslau but to Löwenberg or Lauban to pick up I, making 80,000.

Enemy's invasion would not go much further as in six or eight marches we should have moved III, IV, II, G, to Bautzen—Bischofswerda as well as VIII and VII to Dresden. The advance of these forces into Bohemia must bring back the Austrians out of Silesia.

(*c*) Austrian offensive against Görlitz.

Improbable, has no direct object, leads through barren forests to the lake defiles of the Spree and is a roundabout way to Berlin.

1st Army can meet this move in front through Lübben or can cut the enemy's communications at Spremberg.

(*d*) Prussian offensive.

On June 5th all our nine army corps will have moved up to the border of Saxony and Bohemia. From the military point of view we certainly ought not to postpone action for a single day after June 5th.

By that day Austrians can hardly have transported all their forces to be used against us. But with every succeeding day they will become stronger, and in a few weeks there may be another enemy in Franconia.

The vital thing is to strike down the principal enemy, the one that is ready, before this happens, in which case the Federal Corps will probably never do anything, and if they do, we shall have the means of acting against their flank from Plauen or Eger.

Military considerations then make it desirable that our diplomatic action should come to a conclusion by June 5th.

We shall be on the curve—Zeitz—Torgau—Görlitz—Neisse, 280 English miles long, with 60,000 130,000, 30,000 and 60,000 men.

The quickest way to concentrate any two of these groups, or all of them, is to march forwards, to take the offensive.

If the enemy's main force has moved into Saxony, we can from our positions, in six marches, concentrate 160,000 men round Dresden, either VIII, VII, II, IV, = 120,000, on the left bank of the Elbe, and 70,000 on the right bank, or III, IV, G, and II = 130,000, on the right bank and 60,000 on the left.

If the Austrian main force should be assembled in northern Bohemia the 1st Army would march to its left to deploy on the line Schönlinde—Rumburg—Zittau. I would join at Friedland. In 8 marches 160,000 men.

III. Hoyerswerda—Bautzen—Löbau—Zittau.
II. Senftenberg—Kamenz—Bishofswerda—Rumburg.
IV. Dresden—Stolpen—Schönlinde.
G. In second line Schluckenau.

As in that case in Saxony only the Saxon army is to be got rid of while the above marches are being made; VII and VIII (leaving one division to watch Franconia) can reach Dresden, Bodenbach or Aussig with 45,000 men (two pontoon trains), so that there will be on the line at Tetschen—Friedland (front of 8 miles = 36 English miles) 200,000 men who can be assembled for battle in one march in the neighbourhood of Haida or Gabel.

If the Austrians avoid this collision they would have to give up Saxony and Bohemia without a blow. We should then no doubt meet them at Pardubitz, or even at Olmütz with all their reinforcements, which there will have been ample time to bring up, perhaps altogether 250,000 men. But in that case we too shall have united our 1st and 2nd Armies in Bohemia.

Marginal note of Moltke's on this paper to the effect that Bismarck no longer thought troops needed to watch South Germany on the left bank of the Elbe, and that, therefore, VII and VIII might in due time join the 1st Army.

(Frederick Charles wrote May 25th to Moltke to suggest that it was unlikely that the Austrians would divide their force. Moltke replied) :—

No. 74.

To Prince Frederick Charles.

May 25th.

Agrees. Does not expect the Austrian main attack to be aimed at Silesia, which would not strike the centre of the monarchy and would give Prussia the time to bring up the 1st Army to help the 2nd, either north of the Giant Mountains or, by a bolder and more effectual advance, south of them. More probable an advance of all the available Austrian forces against the 1st Army; but not the whole Austrian army would be available; 50,000 men would have to watch the 2nd Army. At the beginning of June, Benedek could not have more than 130,000 men, the strength of our 1st Army, which on the fourth day will be further strengthened by I. Against the Saxons VII and VIII are an ample force, whether they stand at Zeitz or Düben. The concentration of our forces, which at the beginning are separated in consequence of our geographical position, the direction of our railways and by considerations of defence, can be obtained in a few marches if they move forwards; if they remain where they are it will be more difficult.

(As by the end of May the political situation had not been cleared up it became possible to move II, III and IV nearer to the 2nd Army. Moltke drafted the following order):—

No. 75.

Draft Order.

III. Start June 8.—3 marches to Muskau, June 10.
IV. Start June 5.—6 marches to Hoyerswerda, June 10.
II. Start June 6.—5 marches to Spremberg, June 10.
G. Start June 1.—10 marches to Cottbus, June 10.

(This is part of infantry of G, rest by railway.)

VIII. Start June 7.—4 marches to east of Torgau, June 10.
14th Div. from Zeitz, June 5.—6 marches to west of Torgau, June 10.
13th Div. from Halle.

If on June 11th, when there will be 60,000 men at Torgau and 100,000 at Spremberg, we are still not allowed to invade Saxony (in which case we should deploy five or seven corps in three marches on the line Dresden—Bautzen) but are able to continue our flank march, the 1st Army can be assembled in close quarters round Görlitz, Guard Infantry by train to Halbau by June 14th, and I moved to Greifenberg.

Order (abbreviated).

General von Herwarth is to take command until further notice of VII (except 13th Division) as well as of his own corps. And by June 10th must have his troops quartered between Elster and Mulde. Extension of quarters and date of closing up depend upon events beyond the border.

Bridge to be made above Torgau to enable these troops to assemble on either bank.

1st Army to evacuate the quarters at present assigned to II and IV and to extend its quarters eastwards beyond Muskau by June 10th.

G to march so as to be quartered round Cottbus by June 10th; part of the troops to move by train.

Subordinate commanders to be told only so much of this order as is requisite for its execution; but arrangements for the supply of the troops to be made immediately.

(Orders based on this draft were prepared at the Ministry of War on May 30th, and the movements ordered to begin on June 5th.)

(May 29th, letter from Steinmetz to Moltke complaining that by removing VI from Upper Silesia and posting V at Waldenburg the Austrians are invited to invade Silesia. Long letter full of dissatisfaction. Moltke replied):—

No. 76.

To Steinmetz.

Berlin, June 1st.

Your Excellency has to-day informed me of what you have gathered from utterances of His Royal Highness the Crown Prince and of the views which you have communicated to him. As I have my share in the arrangements made I venture to express to Your Excellency my own views which you may use as you think fit.

We have only one really dangerous enemy, the mainspring of all the other armaments in Germany. This enemy stands there fully armed; it would be a mistake to leave a whole army corps idle in the Rhine Province against an opponent who does not yet exist. We require all our forces against 240,000 Austrians, and all nine army corps (except one division left for the present at Minden) have been brought up.

Austria had six weeks start in her armaments. The essential thing was to stand ready to resist her in the shortest possible time. This could be accomplished only by using *all* the railways *at the same time*. Not more than one corps could be moved along any line and upon none could the railway transport be carried beyond the frontier.

In these given conditions the points of debarkation necessarily formed a cordon along the frontier. No other arrangement could alter this or remove the inevitable geographical circumstance that the Austrians in Bohemia stand upon the inner line of operations between Silesia and the Mark.

An operation directed upon Berlin was the more dangerous inasmuch as no fortress, no line of defence, protects the capital, and our theatre of war has very little depth and very few resources behind it.

Four army corps are posted in Lusatia on the right bank of the Elbe.

For Silesia in the time given only two army corps could be assembled. We can defend Silesia, not in Silesia but only in Bohemia. To place an army in Upper Silesia was not practicable; but that all troops of the line have been already withdrawn from that district was in my opinion neither correct nor as yet required by the circumstances.

The neutrality of Saxony would have had to be discussed not with Saxony but with Austria. It is very far from being advantageous to us, and there have been no negotiations on the subject. The remedy for our scattered points of debarkation —which do not form our strategical deployment—is concentration *to the front*. From our "dispersion" we can in five marches assemble 190,000 men at Dresden, in 9 marches 220,000 men at Schluckenau.

It cannot be said that our army is standing idle. It is not yet there at all. We are still to-day transporting it at the rate of forty trains a day. The railway transport will not be ended until June 5th, and not till then can we accomplish by marching what could not be accomplished by train: the strategical concentration. The first orders for that operation have been given.

The I Army Corps is on the right spot. If we meet the Austrian main force in Saxony or in Northern Bohemia, it would join the 1st Army. If the enemy's main operation is directed against Silesia it is at hand to reinforce the 2nd Army.

For close quarters, which needlessly hampers the troops and the householders, there is no occasion. An ultimatum, even with the shortest delay, of which the army corps can be informed by telegram, will leave them time enough to complete each its own concentration.

The Rhine fortresses are provided with everything necessary. All the available Landwehr reserves have been told off to their functions, and in this respect there are no neglected measures to be made up for.

That all military reasons speak for the initiative is plain. The considerations of another order which have to be weighed are outside the scope of my judgment.

No. 77.
To Bismarck.

May 30th.

In reply to your letter of yesterday evening I permit myself respectfully to enclose the draft for providing 16,000 men for operations in Holstein.

(Details omitted. Marginal note by Moltke: Approved by His Majesty; substance communicated to the Minister of War for the issue of the orders.)

No. 78.

Draft orders for Manteuffel, commanding the force in Holstein.

No. 79.

Notes for Audience of June 3rd.

The Saxon division is concentrated at Dresden on the left bank of the Elbe. In case it is attacked by a superior force it seems that it is to fall back upon the first Austrian corps which stands between Prague and the frontier, mostly on the left bank of the Elbe.

General v. Herwarth will have on June 10th at Torgau—

Of VIII, 24 Battn., 3 Cav. Regts., 16 Bat.
„ VII, 14 „ 2 „ „ 12 „
Altogether 38 „ 5 „ „ 28 „ = 44,000 men,

and will therefore be strong enough to attack, with superior forces after four marches, the Saxons, 20 Battn., 4 Cav. Regts., 10 Bat. = 24,000 men, but these would be supported by

1 Austr. Corps, 28 Battn., 6 Cav. Regts., 20 Bat. = 34,600 men,
Altogether   48 „   10 „   „   30 „ = 58,600 „

so that the Austrians would be in much superior force.

An advance of the first Austrian corps into Saxony to make a stand at Dresden is improbable on account of the simultaneous advance of our 1st Army (see below).

General von Herwarth will therefore presumably compel the Saxons either to fight against twice their strength or immediately to evacuate their country. But after that he will be able only to defend himself in the Erzgebirge until he is reinforced.

The 13th Division can be brought up on two lines of railway in a few days and would raise the strength of the army to 47 Battn., 6 Cav. Regts., 32 Bat. = 54,000 men or about the strength of the united enemy.

But it is uncertain whether the 13th Division can be spared from Minden and therefore necessary to bring up to Saxony the reserve corps from Berlin. That will raise Herwarth's force (without 13th Division) to 62 Battn., 9 Cav. Regts., 44 Bat. = 68,000 men.

The reserve corps cannot reach Dresden before June 24th.

Not till then would the offensive into Bohemia become practicable (leaving 10,000 men in Saxony), but till then also the first Austrian corps would be held.

The rest of the Austrian Northern Army is at this moment, as far as our reports show, on and behind the line Pardubitz—Oswiecim.

Even suppose we assume the Austrian corps now ready (II, IV and perhaps VI) to set off immediately for Northern Bohemia they would not reach the neighbourhood of Zittau in less than 14 days—not before June 16th.

We may therefore calculate with certainty that the 1st Army, which can be deployed on June 15th with 130,000 men on the line Bautzen—Görlitz, will not find a superior enemy before it, not even if the first Austrian corps abandons the Saxons in Prague and moves off to its right.

It follows that our I can be dispensed with at Görlitz as soon as the left wing of the 1st Army approaches this point, that is on June 7th, when I will be completely assembled (the quarters of the 1st Army will be occupied on June 8th).

Accordingly it will be prudent to transfer I by June 10th to the neighbourhood of Hirschberg, from which point it can always, by the road through Schreiberhau, support the advance of the 1st Army if the Austrian main army should really have advanced to the Upper Iser.

But the position of the Austrian army of the North makes this less probable than a principal operation directed against Silesia and therefore our I should without delay be assigned to the 2nd Army (this was approved by the King the same day, June 3rd).

The necessary orders ought to be issued not later than June 5th. If the political situation has been cleared up by June 10th, we can have by June 15th—

> General v. Herwarth with 44,000 men at Dresden.
> Prince Frederick Charles with 130,000 men at Bautzen, Löbau, Görlitz.
> The Crown Prince with 90,000 men at Landeshut.

If we have not to expect a battle in Northern Bohemia the 1st Army will without delay continue its march, in order as soon as possible to come up level with the 2nd Army.

It will depend upon the state of things in Silesia whether this continued march will take place north or south of the Giant Mountains and whether General v. Herwarth will have to reinforce the 1st Army in Bohemia, or the 1st Army directly to reinforce the 2nd in Silesia.

If we may assume that the Austrian first corps will be held fast by General v. Herwarth at the foot of the Erzgebirge (desirable that it should take the offensive) and that at least the second corps observes the approach of our 1st Army so as to protect the most important communications, then there would be left over, to invade Silesia, the fourth, and as far as they would be complete by then, the sixth, eighth, and tenth corps (130,000 men) which would have to weaken themselves by at least 30,000 men in front of Cosel, Neisse, and Glatz.

Thus, the 2nd Army cannot, indeed, prevent the invasion of Upper Silesia, but can very quickly put a stop to the enemy's advance across the line Breslau—Schweidnitz. This army must be reinforced as soon as possible.

Order of the King in Cabinet of June 2nd, 1866, to General Von Moltke.

I send you herewith copy of my order issued this day to the Minister of War, according to which from this time on my orders concerning the operative movements of the concentrated army and its several parts are to be communicated to the Generals in Command through the Chief of the General Staff of the Army, while at the same time the Ministry of War is to be informed by you of whatever takes place.

(Signed) WILLIAM.

No. 80.
To I Army Corps.

June 4th.

To leave its present quarters on June 7th and march towards Hirschberg.

No. 81.
To 1st Army.

June 4th.

That I is to leave Görlitz on June 7th (leaving a garrison till relieved) and march towards Hirschberg and come under Crown Prince.

No. 82.
To 2nd Army.

June 4th.

I to march towards Hirschberg and belong to 2nd Army, which becomes responsible for watching the roads Greiffenberg —Friedland and Hirschberg—Reichenberg.

No. 83.
To Chief of Staff of Elbe Army.

Berlin, June 3rd.

Reported to-day that Saxons have five battalions and a cavalry regiment on right bank of Elbe, headquarters Moritzburg, place of assembly Pulsnitz.

The rest of the Saxon army is on the left bank about Wilsdruff and Dresden.

I think that when we invade Saxony we can neglect the detachment on the right bank.

The first Austrian Army Corps is between Prague and the frontier with three brigades on the left bank. It is not likely to advance against Saxony, as, when we advance against Dresden, our 1st Army will probably march upon Bautzen. The Austrian corps is probably meant to wait for the Saxons to fall back upon it at the southern foot of the Erzgebirge.

Learns that the troops quartered between Torgau and Elsterwerda, though welcomed by the inhabitants, are yet a burden to them; thinks that this might be lightened by quartering some in the district Eilenburg—Düben. . . . Hanover neither friendly nor hostile, better for us if she were hostile, though that would prevent us bringing up the 13th Division through Halle. But the reserve corps will assemble at Berlin between the 8th and 12th of June.

No. 84.
To the same.

June 4th.

Now reported that Saxons will assemble on right bank at Bischofswerda—Bautzen. The burdensomeness of quarters does not matter much as we shall probably not have much longer to wait. Let me know where the bridge above Torgau is placed, and whether it is finished, and on what day VII and VIII can be ready on one bank of the Elbe.

(As it seemed probable that Hanover would take sides against Prussia, arrangements were made to keep troops to deal with her forces. For this purpose, besides the troops in Schleswig-Holstein and certain garrison regiments, the 13th Division was told off. Moltke's orders were contained in—

Nos. 85 and 86.
To Vogel von Falckenstein. Münster.
(Text not reproduced.)

(The deployment as hitherto ordered was completed on June 10th, but there was then a partial movement, of which the origin is explained in the correspondence between Moltke and Blumenthal.)

Blumenthal to Moltke.

Headquarters, Fürstenstein, June 8th.

As Your Excellency will have gathered from the conspectus of our information sent from here yesterday, our conjecture has almost attained certainty, that, if war breaks out, the Austrians intend to advance through Upper Silesia past the fortresses upon Breslau.

The only question is which route they will take for their main force, the left, the right, or both banks of the Oder? In each of these cases I think the 2nd Army should be packed behind the Neisse between Grottkau—Neisse and Patschkau, with an advance guard towards Neustadt and Ziegenhals. This defensive position supported by the fortress is fitted to delay the enemy and in favourable circumstances for an offensive advance against him.

We therefore intend to start from here on the 11th, and to be concentrated on the Neisse not later than the 16th. But unfortunately we are obliged, in the first instance, to leave in this region a division (or a strong brigade) as it is still after all an open question whether the enemy will not advance on this side with strong forces against Schweidnitz and Breslau. Yesterday, therefore, being at Schweidnitz, on the spot, I ordered a few field works, and hope that the division, if it has to fall back so far, can hold its ground a few days against superior forces.

For the protection of Breslau we cannot, for the present, do more, and must leave the defence of the town against a cavalry raid on the right bank of the Oder to the supplementary reserve troops there and to whatever Stolberg's detachment can do (detachment of 6 battalions and 8 squadrons Landwehr, in Upper Silesia).

You will understand that in these circumstances we are very anxious to be reinforced. . . . We should be much easier if the Guard Corps, or most of it, could be sent to Brieg, and this district protected by the 1st Army.

If the enemy advances on the left bank of the Oder we shall hold our ground, and if he comes with superior force shall accept battle. If he comes on both banks we shall hope to beat him in detail, and Stolberg will impede his march upon Breslau. If his main force moves by the right bank I do not yet clearly see what we shall do. I can hardly think he will be bold enough to push in between us and the Russian frontier; perhaps that is the very thing that we ought to wish for, and I am considering how we can increase our means of crossing the Oder.

What would be most disagreeable to me would be, if in spite of all our information to the contrary, he advanced in great force by Landeshut and Waldenburg. . . .

(The above letter crossed with the following telegram, from which it may be inferred that Moltke had been induced by the presence of the Crown Prince at Potsdam to consider the questions raised in Blumenthal's letter):—

No. 87.

Telegram to Blumenthal.

Berlin, June 8th.

Think this over: if another Army Corps were sent to you by railway where would you wish it to go? Greiffenberg, Liegnitz, Breslau or where? Reply to-morrow morning.

(Blumenthal telegraphed back):—

Fürstenstein, June 9th, 6 a.m.

The corps would best be sent to Brieg. Explanation in my letter already sent.

(To Blumenthal's letter Moltke replied)—

No. 88.

Telegram to Blumenthal.

Berlin, June 9th, 11.56 a.m.

As His Majesty reserves for himself the direction of operations, important changes in the position of the army must not be made without His Majesty's approval. Agree substantially with your views.

(Blumenthal replied with the following telegram):—

Fürstenstein, June 9th, 4 p.m.

In consequence of your telegram the march to the Neisse suspended. A proposal on the subject goes to-night to the King. If you can, pray inform me of decision by telegraph to-morrow.

(The Crown Prince's proposal was contained in a letter from him to the King.)

Headquarters, Fürstenstein, June 9th.

The letter is a paraphrase of Blumenthal's letter of June 8th, and concludes :—Being convinced of the urgency and necessity of the movement I feel it my duty respectfully to propose to Your Majesty to approve of the prompt march of the 2nd Army to the Neisse, and to inform me by telegraph of your approval.

(Meanwhile, Moltke has written to Blumenthal as follows) :—

No. 89.
To Blumenthal.

Berlin, June 9th.

Do not infer from my telegram of to-day that it is the intention, once the operations of the army have begun in the face of the enemy, to restrict them by instructions from above. My whole endeavour would be directed to preventing this. But the general instructions whether an army is to proceed offensively or defensively, whether it is to advance or retire, can be issued only by His Majesty, for the movements of the one army must necessarily be connected with those of the other.

The idea of taking position with the 2nd Army behind the Neisse after leaving a stronger or weaker detachment at Landeshut or Schweidnitz seems to me in and by itself quite correct. This strong position between the fortress of Neisse and the county of Glatz directly protects Breslau and the greater part of Silesia, and the possibility of taking the offensive so soon as the offensive is permissible also secures Upper Silesia. Enterprises of the enemy on the right bank of the Oder can never be decisive.

But a measure of that kind must needs coincide with a simultaneous advance of the 1st Army. That army's left wing has occupied Görlitz, and its union with the 2nd Army can be accomplished in a few marches after the 1st Army has deployed on the line Dresden—Görlitz. This advance into Saxony is, however, for the present not permitted for political (or unpolitical) reasons. If the 1st Army remains stationary in its extended quarters in Lusatia, then there comes about a complete separation from the 2nd so soon as the 2nd by itself makes five marches forward. I submit for your consideration whether it would not meet the circumstances in the first instance to occupy the proposed position on the Neisse with the VI Corps alone.

The possible retreat of this corps, if it should become

necessary, can hardly be endangered, and might prepare for the advance of larger forces. But this must be decided by the Commander of the (2nd) Army. You are quite right that the Austrian position points to an invasion of Upper Silesia by way of Neisse with large masses which are assembled in the triangle Gabel, Olmütz, Oderberg. The offensive advance of the 1st Army into Bohemia would best give you breathing-space, and would very probably draw upon itself the Third and Eighth Austrian Corps as well as the First.

But if this offensive advance cannot be obtained there remains in my opinion only the direct reinforcement of the Silesian Army.

The Guard Corps will arrive to-morrow in its cantonments round Cottbus after heavy marches. The Commander of the 1st Army will be instructed to-morrow to extend these cantonments towards Sommerfeld and Sorau, and, as there are still nine battalions of the corps at Berlin—Potsdam, it will then be possible, by using 16 trains a day, to move the corps to the point at which, in the immediate future, its presence may prove to be necessary.

P.S.—Your telegram of 4 p.m. to-day just arrived.

I read to-day to His Majesty from your letter of the 8th instant all that concerns the position on the Neisse, expressed myself entirely in its favour, but at the same time pointed out the necessity of the simultaneous advance of the 1st Army.

(Royal Order of June 10th, approving of the march to the Neisse, and of the reinforcement of the 2nd Army by the Guard Corps, which is to be moved by railway to Brieg.)

No. 90.
Telegram to Blumenthal.

Berlin, June 10th, 2.10 p.m.

Proposal of 9th approved on all points. More by letter to-morrow.

No. 91.
To Blumenthal.

Berlin, June 11th, Evening.

The proposal of the Crown Prince has been approved, and the disadvantage arising from the advance of the 2nd Army

—the disadvantage of a new separation from the 1st Army —has been as far as possible made up for by the 1st Army receiving to-day the order to continue its flank march towards Görlitz.

You know that according to my wish the 1st Army and General von Herwarth should have moved into Saxony. Their front of 25 (German) miles would thereby have been reduced to the line 10 (German) miles long from Dresden to Görlitz. They would, in all probability, in their further advance into Bohemia, have drawn upon themselves two or three Austrian Corps, and thus have indirectly procured a very considerable relief for the 2nd Army.

But we must not reckon with our wishes and our hopes, but with given magnitudes. The permission for this advance cannot be expected during the next eight days, for non-military but all the same very important reasons. This time should not be lost in waiting. By the 18th, when you will be upon the Neisse, the 1st Army will reach cantonments stretching from Niesky to Greiffenberg and Hirschberg (unless before then concentration on Görlitz should become necessary). The 1st Army at the crossroads of Görlitz will be available either for operations in Silesia or for an advance into Saxony, and even, without touching Saxony, into Bohemia.

The advance of the whole army by way of Friedland into Bohemia could be effective only if there were already in Bohemia a portion of the enemy of something like corresponding strength. If that is not the case, this indirect assistance comes too late to be effective. A vigorous leader like Benedek is not sure to be thereby induced to give up his operations in Silesia. There he has Hungary and the Galician Railway behind him, and will lead all his forces against whatever he has in front of him. The Austrians, taught by the ill-success of their turning movements and positions in reserve, have probably fallen into the opposite extreme of "going for the enemy." It is to be hoped that our infantry fire will cool this heat; but we may count upon them coming up shoulder to shoulder.

As long as the Brigade Kalik remains at Altona nothing will happen. But it may move off at any moment, and the next day we shall have an ultimatum. As we are leaving the initiative to the Austrians they will have finished their concentration before (sending their ultimatum). I think that then they can appear before Neisse in 24 hours with II, X, VI, and perhaps a part of IV, about 100,000 men.

Don't you think it would be better to take a position not on the river, but behind it? In passing the fortress of Neisse the attack must weaken itself by 15,000 or 20,000 men. The Neisse can be walked through nearly everywhere, and is made difficult only by the Muhlgraben, which, however, covers only a part of the space. Intrenchments, as a rule, do not meet the case because the enemy comes another way than the one expected.

The I Austrian Corps cannot co-operate in an attack on Silesia, but Benedek can very well bring up III and VIII for his offensive a few days later. He would then, certainly, have 100,000 men after deductions for the fortresses.

I think you will share the view that nothing would be more disadvantageous than to want to fight on the Neisse against a decided superiority, if four or five days later we can assemble seven corps on the line Schweidnitz—Breslau.

The difficulty is only to get to know exactly what we really have against us. Unless we learn beforehand that another Austrian corps beside I has moved off to protect Bohemia, I think it certain that you will have six corps in front of you—it is true that they will not be all at hand on the first day, and if a retreat is necessary, as it will follow the mountains, it will certainly give the opportunity for victorious rear guard actions.

You will judge better on the spot than I can from here. I should merely like to warn you against letting yourself be carried away into fighting without regard to the circumstances. No doubt it is easier to advise resistance at any price than to advise a retirement, however necessary.

I hope we shall have seven more days to finish our deployment.

(Blumenthal replied on June 13th, discussing his plans. Royal Order of June 10th, assigning the Guard Corps to the 2nd Army and instructing the II Army Corps to move into its place in quarters round Cottbus.)

No. 92.

Order to Guard Corps.

June 10th.

Guard Corps to belong to 2nd Army, but to arrange its quarters in conjunction with 1st Army.

Frederick Charles to the King.

Headquarters, Muskau, June 11th.

Suggests that the 1st Army proper (III, IV and Cavalry Corps), should march towards 2nd Army.

The King replied on the 12th, that the orders for the 1st Army to move to its left had been sent off on the 11th.

No. 93.
To the Commander of the 2nd Army.

Berlin, June 11th.

His Majesty has orderd the 1st Army (II, III and IV) to take quarters between Niesky and Hirschberg, and the necessary marches are to be begun within the next few days.

General v. Herwarth is to remain until further notice on the Elbe.

No. 94.
To Herwarth.

Berlin, June 11th.

Paraphrase of 93.

No. 95.
To Major-General v. Stülpnagel.
(1st Army.)

As long as six corps stand before the Crown Prince the main thing is to give him direct support. To invade Bohemia with 120,000 men with a view to disengage him indirectly would not affect a determined opponent soon enough.

Reports make it probable that the Austrian II Corps has been sent to support I in Bohemia. That simplifies the Crown Prince's situation, and it might be worth while to hunt the two corps in Bohemia, with superior forces.

But I do not think it justified, upon a by no means guaranteed report, to modify the leftward march of the 1st Army, a part of which can always be sent to Bautzen—Zittau, even from Görlitz—Greiffenberg.

The Austrian proposal at the Diet has been accepted to-day,

so that we are pretty certain to march into Saxony, presumably on the 17th. The telegram which you will then receive will merely announce that a part of the 1st Army must invade Lusatia. How much it would be left for the commander to determine, and he must be guided by what he has in front of him in Northern Bohemia.

If, as is desirable, we can assume there more than two of the enemy's corps, Herwarth will, if possible, be brought up from the Elbe to the right wing of the 1st Army. If there is nothing important in Bohemia, the point will be to reinforce the Crown Prince, which will have been accomplished if the 5th and 6th Divisions relieve his detachment at Landeshut. If time fails nothing will be left but to let the 2nd Army fall back on the 1st.

(The leftward march, No. 93, was not fully carried out. Austria proposed in the Diet the mobilization of all the non-Prussian forces of the Federation. The vote was fixed for the 14th, and as it was a foregone conclusion, measures were taken in Prussia to declare war against and to invade the hostile States, above all Saxony, Hanover and Electoral Hesse. For this purpose Moltke issued the orders):—

No. 96.
To Herwarth.

Berlin, June 12th.

Be ready on June 16th to invade Saxony by the left bank of Elbe. The reserve corps, which will be sent on as soon as possible, comes under your orders. The 1st Army will advance to Bautzen—Görlitz, so that the Saxon detachment on the right bank is sure to retire, and an advance of the I Austrian Corps into Saxony is improbable.

No. 97.
Telegram to Vogel v. Falckenstein.

Berlin, June 12th.

13th Division to be immediately collected at Minden.

No. 98.
To Vogel v. Falckenstein.

Berlin, June 12th.

Confirms telegram, and explains arrangements for invading Hanover.

No. 99.
To Major-General v. Beyer, Wetzlar.

Berlin, June 12th.

Beyer is to have his troops collected and ready to attack Hesse or Nassau on June 16th.

No. 100.
To Prince Frederick Charles, Muskau.

Berlin, June 13th.

Herwarth may invade Saxony on the 16th, on the left bank Prince Frederick Charles to be ready in that case to move an army corps to Bautzen or Löbau, which will compel the withdrawal of the Saxon detachment from the right bank.

No. 101.
To Crown Prince.

Berlin, June 13th.

Repeats substance of 100. Crown Prince to be careful not to be drawn into conflict with superior numbers before he can be supported by the 1st Army.

No. 102.
To Manteuffel.

Berlin, June 15th.

He is to be ready to have his 13,000 or 14,000 men at Altona prepared for anything on June 15th.

(The Austrian proposal was accepted by the Diet on June 14th, but Moltke thought he would not be allowed to invade the hostile States before June 17th.)

No. 103.
To Manteuffel.

Berlin, June 14th.

See what you can do to be ready to get your force across to Harburg.

No. 104.
To Beyer.

Berlin, June 14th.

On Sunday 17th, at noon, you are, in any case, to invade Hesse, unless you previously receive an order to stop you.

No. 105.
To Herwarth, Falckenstein and Manteuffel.

Telegram.

Berlin, June 14th, 10 p.m.

"Invasion not before June 17th."

(On June 14th, at 6.45 p.m., Bismarck wrote to ask whether Manteuffel had already been ordered to cross the Elbe, and urging that Beyer should start for Cassel on the evening of the 15th. Moltke replied.)

No. 106.
To Bismarck.

Berlin, June 14th, 11 p.m.

Notified Manteuffel that he must cross the Elbe to-morrow; Beyer is quite ready. If the diplomatic questions are put to-morrow at Cassel he can invade on the 16th.

(Moltke now learns that ultimatum sent to Dresden, Hanover, and Cassel expires on June 15th at midnight. He, therefore, issues the orders for invasion to take place on June 16th.)

No. 107.
To Herwarth, Torgau.

Telegram.

Berlin, June 15th, between 6.30 and 7.30 a.m.

Diplomatic decision to-day. You herewith receive His Majesty's command to invade Kingdom of Saxony to-morrow, Saturday the 16th, at 6 a.m., unless, meantime, you receive contrary instructions from here or from the Ambassador at Dresden. Report receipt of this.

No. 108.
To 1st Army, Görlitz.
Telegram.
Berlin, June 15th, between 6.30 and 7.30 a.m.

Herwarth will invade Saxony on left bank of Elbe at 6 a.m. to morrow, Saturday. The 1st Army is at the same time to occupy the district of Löbau with its nearest troops. Possible invasion of Austrian territory not to be undertaken without special order. Report receipt.

No. 109.
To Falckenstein at Minden.
Telegram.
Berlin, June 15th, between 6.30 and 7.30 a.m.

Diplomatic decision to-day. You hereby receive His Majesty's command to invade Kingdom of Hanover, at 6 a.m. to-morrow, Saturday 16th, unless, meantime, you receive instructions to the contrary from here or from the Ambassador at Hanover. Report receipt. Copy gone to Holsteina. Manteuffel crosses Elbe to-morrow.

No. 110.
To Manteuffel, Altona.
Telegram.
Berlin, June 15th, between 6.30 and 7.30 a.m.

Order just been sent to Falckenstein (text of 109). Your Excellency herewith receives His Majesty's commands also to invade Hanover to-morrow.

No. 111.
To Beyer, Wetzlar.
Telegram.
Berlin, June 15th, between 6.30 and 7.30 a.m.

Diplomatic decision to-day. You receive herewith His Majesty's orders to start your march to Cassel at 6 a.m. to-morrow, Saturday, the 16th, unless, meantime, you receive contrary instructions from here or from the Ambassador at Cassel. Report receipt.

No. 112.
To Herwarth, Falckenstein, Manteuffel and Beyer.
Telegram.
Berlin, June 15th, 10.30 p.m.

On invading issue soothing proclamation to inhabitants that we are not coming as enemies. Private property to be strictly spared. State property to be treated as our own.

(During the night 15th to 16th war was declared.)

No. 113.
To Commander of 1st Army and to Herwarth, Falckenstein, Manteuffel and Beyer.
Telegram.
June 16th.

War has been declared against Hesse, Hanover and Saxony. If on their territories Austrian troops are met they are to be requested to withdraw, and if they refuse, to be treated as enemies.

No. 114.
To 1st Army.
Telegram.
Berlin, June 16th.

Same as No. 112.

No. 115.
To Vogel v. Falckenstein.
Telegram.
Berlin, June 16th.

Beyer is advancing from Wetzlar against Cassel. Hanoverian troops said to be moving to Göttingen. Report receipt.

No. 116.
To Beyer.
Telegram.
Berlin, June 16th.

Hanoverian troops moving to Göttingen. Report receipt.

No. 117.

To Falckenstein, Manteuffel, and Beyer.
Telegram.

Berlin, June 16th.

Receipt of cipher and other telegrams must always be immediately acknowledged by telegram.

Addition for Beyer:

Destroy Frankfort Railway at Nauheim. King of Hanover left last night for Göttingen.

(On the 14th it was reported that the Austrian II Corps, hitherto observing Glatz, had gone off into Bohemia to the district north of Prague, and that only IV Corps at Hohenstädt remained available in the first line against Silesia, with X and VI in second line behind it at Olmütz-Weisskirchen, and in third line III and VIII at Brünn and east of Brünn. Thereupon Moltke drafted the following outline plan for the first movements of the army):—

No. 118.

Berlin, probably June 14th.

Dresden to be entrenched.

One division of Herwarth occupies the passes of the Erzegebirge towards Teplitz.

To be reinforced by the small contingents and whatever can gradually be made available; if hard pressed by Saxons and II Austrian Corps, falls back at Dresden across the Elbe, or possibly towards Torgau.

4th Battalions assemble at Berlin.

Herwarth marches to Stolpen to join on to the 1st Army; in four or five marches 145,000 men between Niemes and Turnau.

The I Corps from Patschkau *viâ* Glatz or Landeshut to Trautenau; after six or seven marches 180,000 men at Gitschen.

Crown Prince offensive against Hohenstadt.

(Theodore v. Bernhardi reported on June 9th a conversation which took place on June 6th with la Marmora to the following effect: The Italian General has maintained great reserve concerning his plan of campaign against Austria. He was apparently convinced that the task of the Italian Army could be carried out only by an offensive war, but he conceived of the attack as consisting simply in gaining possession of the quadrilateral by siege. For this purpose he proposed to cross the Mincio with the main army and attack the Austrian forces in front, while against their flank only a subordinate army, under General Cialdini, was to advance from the Lower Po. Thereupon Bernhardi pointed out that it was much easier to strike at the retreat of the Austrians from the quadrilateral if a mere demonstration were made upon their front, while the main army moved through the Polesina into Venetia. La Marmora rejected this proposal as too daring.

Bernhardi received the impression that an energetic and effective action of the Italian army, such as would draw off considerable Austrian forces from the northern theatre of war, was not to be expected and could not be counted upon. To his letter Moltke replied)—

No. 119.

To Bernhardi.

Berlin, June 15th.

From your very interesting letter of the 9th instant I perceive with regret that we have little to hope from Italy's co-operation. It is remarkable that they should fail to see at Florence that the quadrilateral is easier to gain by beating the Austrians in the open field than by besieging the fortresses. This latter undertaking may last for months, nay, for years, without leading to the goal. An advance upon Padua cuts the enemy's arteries. It compels him to move out, because he would have nothing to eat. But to do that Cialdini's force is much too weak.

But quite apart from these obvious considerations, and presuming that the gigantic task of besieging Mantua or Verona is crowned with a hardly credible success—have they forgotten that at the time of the first French Empire, Austria had been driven back much further than would be the case if she now lost Venetia, and that this same Austria was yet able again to force Italy under her yoke. Do they not see on the Arno that nothing but a substantial weakening of the Empire gives any guarantee of being able to maintain a conquest even if it has been made? . . .

My hope is that King Victor Emanuel, who is himself both statesman and soldier, will see things in another light, and that at the last decisive moment he will lead his fine and numerous army through the Polesina, will cut through the most important communications of the quadrilateral, will surround Venice by land and sea, and push on against the heart of the Austrian monarchy.

PART III.

THE WAR.

I.—The Campaign against Austria and Saxony.

(On June 16th the 1st and Elbe Armies invaded the kingdom of Saxony. In the evening General Herwarth telegraphed from Riesa to Berlin to ask whether and in what direction the 1st Army had crossed the Frontier. He added that according to reports Bavarian troops had entered Saxony and were advancing against his right flank, Moltke immediately replied) :—

No. 120.
Telegram to Herwarth.

Berlin, June 16th.

8th Division at Löbau. Rest of 1st Army close behind. Bavarians as yet hardly ready for operations. Austrian reinforcements possible.

(Major-General v. Stülpnagel, Q.M.G. of 1st Army, inquired on June 16th from Görlitz whether on this day further orders for the 1st Army were to be expected or whether it might act independently on the 17th. Moltke replied) :—

No. 121.
Telegram to Stülpnagel.

Berlin, June 16th.

No orders from here but bear in mind that Austrian territory may not yet be touched, that Herwarth has to be supported and that it may be desirable for him to join on to the right wing of the 1st Army. Herwarth is advancing on left bank of Elbe and cannot reach Dresden until the 18th.

(On June 17th the 1st and Elbe Armies continued their advance towards Dresden up to the line Meissen—Bautzen. On the evening of this day General Moltke telegraphed) :—

No. 122.
Telegram to Herwarth.

Berlin, June 17th, 7 p.m.

Bavarian Ambassador asked for his passports to-day. Railway to Hof to be interrupted if possible beyond Chemnitz. (With a view to securing and defending Saxon districts already occupied Moltke wrote):—

No. 123.
Telegram to Military Governor of Prussian Saxony at Magdeburg.

A detachment to be sent to Leipzig.

No. 124.
To Roon.

Suggestion for providing 10,000 troops to occupy Saxony.

No. 125.
Telegram to Herwarth.

That a battalion has been ordered from Torgau to Leipzig.

(On June 18th Moltke wrote to Stülpnagel the following letter, which is not in the official correspondence but in Lettow-Vorbeck, II, Second Edition, page 98.)

Berlin, June 18th.

I have to thank you for yesterday communicating to me the excellent arrangements of the 1st Army for a closer concentration. You are probably aware that General Herwarth to-day enters Dresden, General Falckenstein is to-day entering the city of Hanover, and to-morrow morning General Beyer enters Cassel—Unfortunately all without fighting.

The Hanoverian troops have escaped in great haste by railway to Göttingen, the Hessians, 400 men per battalion, to Bebra. Where the Saxons are we don't yet know here to-day; I hope that the 14th Division will push them away from Chemnitz. We also do not know here whether Bavarian troops have really entered Saxony. You see that information is scarce here perhaps because those on the spot have none. The despatch of 4,000 Austrians to Dresden does not seem to have taken place any more than that of 6,000 to Zittau.

Three of the Princes who have built upon Austria's help have probably paid for it by now with the loss of their lands, without the Austrians having even drawn the sword. Possible that it yet comes to a fight in Saxony but if not North Germany has been conquered without a shot having been fired.

But this success is real only if we know how to maintain it and the decision lies in Bohemia. It is very hard at present to decide whether the 1st Army should reinforce the 2nd or the 2nd the 1st. It depends on whether the Austrians turn their main forces against Silesia or against Lusatia. We know that the Fourth and Sixth Austrian Corps are still to-day opposite Glatz and Upper Silesia, that the Second and First have been brought up to Northern Bohemia and that since June 11th there has been much movement, but for all our spies we do not know whether the 3rd, 8th and 10th have moved off.

It is thus very easy to order movements that will afterwards turn out unsuitable and we must needs wait for more light. If we learn that five corps have gone to Bohemia then the I Army Corps must be brought up through Hirschberg to the left wing of the 1st Army and the Crown Prince take the offensive with his three corps. If it turns out that only the First and Second Austrian Corps are in Bohemia it would be necessary directly to reinforce the Crown Prince and to go forward from Lusatia.

It seems to me not improbable that Benedek will take the decisive direction of Berlin in order to unite again with his First and Second Corps.

For me, therefore, the advance of General v. Herwarth is not the conquest of Saxony, but a deployment upon the line Dresden—Görlitz and the junction with the right wing of the 1st Army. It would be very unwelcome if the retirement of the Saxons not to Bohemia but to a Bavarian army in Franconia were to draw off General Herwarth from the Elbe.

By degrees our conglomerate opponents are assembling on the Main. I hope that very soon 36,000 men will take the offensive against them, which ought to be the best way of protecting our Rhine province.

I am thinking day and night only how we can make as strong as possible that one of our two armies which the Austrian main army will attack. Happily each of them is from 130,000 to 150,000 strong, and such an army takes some beating. As soon as ever General Herwarth becomes available, that moment I think we will, in God's name, march into Bohemia.

(On June 18th the Elbe Army occupied Dresden, where

it rested on the 19th. In the night of the 18th to 19th Moltke telegraphed) :—

No. 126.
Telegram to Colonel v. Schlotheim, Riesa.
Berlin, June 19th, 12.5 a.m.

No report come. Has General Herwarth entered Dresden ? Where are the Saxons ? Have any Austrians joined them ?

(Schlotheim replied on 19th from Dresden that 16th Division had entered Dresden on 18th, that no Saxon or Austrian troops had been met but that Bavarian troops were said to have come to Hof on 18th.

With the occupation of Saxony the first stage of the campaign was ended. The invasion of Bohemia by the whole army was to follow immediately. For it, Moltke drew up the following brief plan) :—

No. 127.
Berlin, no date (probably June 19th).

The reports coming in point to a concentration of the Austrian main forces towards Northern Bohemia.

The 1st Army takes the offensive thither.

The 2nd Army has to draw nearer to it in order to effect a junction by the offensive into Bohemia.

In Saxony is to remain a division of General v. d. Mülbe.

General Herwarth to march on 20th to Stolpen, on 25th union at Gitschin of 150,000 men.

The 2nd Army by its offensive holds fast at Neisse and Grulich at least two Austrian corps and debouches with two corps.

(This draft forms the basis of the following telegram) :—

No. 128.
To the Commander of the 2nd Army.
Telegram.
Berlin, June 19th, 6.30 p.m.

United offensive into Bohemia ordered. I Army Corps to be put in march towards Landeshut to-morrow the 20th. One corps to remain at Neisse. Written order to-morrow.

(This telegram was directly followed by) :—

No. 129.
To the Commander of 2nd Army.

Berlin, June 19th.

The Saxon Army has withdrawn to Bohemia. All reports agree that the First and Second Austrian Army Corps are close to the Saxon border on both sides of the Elbe, the Third Corps moving towards Pardubitz, the Eighth towards Brünn.

The Fourth Corps also seems to be extending westwards.

All this leads to the conclusion that the enemy's main force is concentrating towards Bohemia.

It is the will of His Majesty the King that, before this can be completely accomplished the 1st Army should take the offensive.

General v. Herwarth has received orders to leave behind on the left bank of the Elbe only a division, shortly to be reinforced, but with the rest of his force to move off to-morrow, the 20th, in the direction of Stolpen and to join on to the right wing of the 1st Army. He comes under the orders of His Royal Highness Prince Frederick Charles.

The 1st Army is then immediately to begin its forward march and has to keep close to the mountains with its right wing.

Although this advance shortens the distance between the two armies yet in the now changed conditions a movement of the 2nd Army to meet the 1st is necessary to hasten the union.

The I Army Corps is therefore immediately to be set in motion towards Landeshut in order, in case of need, to be able to reinforce the 1st Army through Schreiberhau or through Trautenau.

Only one army corps must for the present remain upon the Neisse. The two others are to be so echelonned level with Glatz and Frankenstein on the different roads that the greater port of the Army can be further assembled in the shortest time at Landeshut or at Neisse or that in case of need the offensive can be taken from the county of Glatz.

The Commander of the 1st Army has received a communication identical with this and the Commander of the 2nd Army is to remain in constant understanding with him.

The position of the corps and divisions under your orders is everyday briefly to be reported to me by telegram.

No. 130.

To Herwarth, Dresden.

Telegram.

Berlin, June 19th, 7.30 p.m.

Your troops are to march off to Stolpen on the 20th. A division of the reserve corps and two batteries horse artillery of the VII Corps remain at Dresden. Latter intended for another destination.

(To secure Dresden against attack from the west were given orders) :—

Nos. 131 and 132.

Arranging for the fortification of Dresden.

(On June 21st General v. Stülpnagel telegraphed to ask whether I Army Corps belonged to the 1st or 2nd Army. Moltke telegraphed) :—

No. 133.

To Stülpnagel.

Berlin, June 21st, p.m.

I Corps belongs to 2nd Army.

March direction of 1st Army to be communicated to me as soon as possible.

No. 134.

To Blumenthal.

Berlin, June 21st, 8.10 p.m.

I Army Corps belongs to the 2nd Army. How has march of I Army Corps been arranged in accord as ordered with 1st Army ? Reply to-morrow.

(Blumenthal replied I Army Corps would be on 22nd at Waldenburg and would there rest on 23rd.

Meantime the apprehension hitherto felt that the Austrian main army would advance against Upper Silesia had proved groundless and all indications pointed to its assembling in Bohemia. Consequently the 2nd Army became available for action in concert with the 1st ; only one army corps had to remain on the Neisse to protect Silesia. On June 22nd was issued the following order) :—

No. 135.
To the Commanders of the 1st and 2nd Armies.
Telegram.
Berlin, June 22nd, p.m.

His Majesty orders both armies to enter Bohemia and to seek their union in the direction of Gitschin. The VI Corps remains available at Neisse.

No. 136.
To the Commander of the 2nd Army.
Berlin, June 22nd.

His Majesty's order to move into Bohemia has been given in to-day's cypher telegram just sent off.

The direction of Gitschin has been given for the eventual union of the two armies, because the distances, the communications by road and the railways make it seem suitable.

Of course this does not mean that Gitschin must be reached in any circumstances; that depends upon the course of events.

According to all the intelligence that we have here it is quite improbable that the Austrian main force could be assembled ready in Northern Bohemia in the next few days. As we are taking the initiative there might easily be an opportunity of attacking them with superior forces while they are divided, and of following up the victory in another direction. All the same the union of all our forces for the decisive battle must all the time be kept in view. The Commander of each army from the moment when he is facing the enemy must employ the troops entrusted to him according to his own judgment and the requirements of the situation, but in so doing must always consider the situation of his fellow army. Mutual support between the two will be facilitated by their continuously comparing notes.

Although the VI Army Corps is intended in the first instance for the defence of Silesia, yet it is left open for this corps to take the offensive. An early and vigorous demonstration from Neisse, or from the County of Glatz, against the very important railway line Pardubitz—Prerau will undoubtedly keep away at least one Austrian army corps from Bohemia.

Care must be taken as the advance proceeds to protect or in case of need to restore, the railway Zittau—Reichenberg, &c., as well as the telegraphic communications.

No. 137.

To the Commander of the 1st Army.

Berlin, June 22nd.

The text of No. 136 with this addition: As the weaker 2nd Army has the more difficult task of issuing from the mountains, it is the more incumbent on the 1st Army, as soon as ever its junction with the force of General v. Herwarth has been affected, to shorten the crisis by its swift advance.

(*From Lettow-Vorbeck*, Vol. II, Second Edition, p. 118. *To Stülpnagel.*)

Berlin, June 22nd.

Thanks for the two letters of yesterday. From the table showing the marches of the I Army Corps, it appears that this corps could not reach Reichenberg in less than six days. Besides, the difficult defile on the Upper Iser has been entrenched by the enemy. If you wish to wait so long for direct reinforcement by an army corps perhaps two of the enemy's army corps would be able to come up in the same time. A better effect will therefore undoubtedly be produced indirectly by the offensive advance of the 2nd Army, which His Majesty has to-day sanctioned. This will draw upon itself a portion, perhaps too large a portion, of the enemy.

It is to be hoped that the advantages of the initiative will fall to us in Bohemia, as they have done in Hesse, Saxony, and Hanover; I think that you will hit upon the heads of columns and have the opportunity of nice actions.

Perhaps your advance guard will be already reporting that there is no need to concentrate such important forces against Reichenberg. Such a concentration, except when it leads directly to a decisive battle, is in itself a calamity. I do not think that the Austrians will be very strong there, but I am not without apprehension that General Herwarth on his march up to you from the Elbe will be attacked on his right flank by the I and II Austrian Corps. Would it not be advisable to support him with at least the 8th Division by letting it halt at St. Pankraz until he comes up? If the Austrians came on in this fashion it would probably be worth while to use your very superior forces to drive them against the Elbe and destroy them, taking care, of course, to guard your own left flank. From my official letter of to-day you will see that though the direction of Gitschin must determine your movement as a whole, yet you may go out of your way for a tangible success if you get it. Only the departure from the general direction must not be a blow in the air. In presence of an actual tactical victory all considerations of strategy disappear. In any case the Crown Prince cannot cross the frontier before the 26th.

(On June 22nd, Blumenthal asked for a rest day for the 2nd Army and permission to move VI Army Corps into the County of Glatz. Moltke replied) :—

No. 138.
Telegram to Blumenthal.
Berlin, June 23rd, 9 a.m.

Rest day and use to be made of VI Corps entirely at the discretion of Commander of 2nd Army.

(This was followed by the following letter) :—

No. 139.
To Blumenthal.
Berlin, June 24th.

You will see from my official letter of the 22nd (136) and from my telegram (138) that it rests entirely with the Army Commander to bring up the VI Corps. Indeed I think this measure much to the point, and hope that the Austrian demonstration of an advance upon Glatz was what you wanted, and that it suggested your proposal. An offensive counterstroke from Grulich upon Hohenstadt would be very effective and perhaps give you relief at Nachod. The V Corps has there a difficult task : to cover the flank of the whole army. It may easily be that General Steinmetz must retire northwards upon Braunau. The Guard Corps would have to guarantee his being supported; you have only to see to it that the leading is right and correct.

The intelligence is in a bad way in spite of all our trouble. If it proves true that the Austrians are concentrating at Jungbunzlau the union of our army would be assured if only the advance from both sides is quick. A great decision is coming. God will not desert us. I hardly get to bed at all; since yesterday evening we are negotiating with the Hanoverian army for capitulation. Weak scratch detachments of garrison troops at Eisenach and Gotha have hitherto prevented them from forcing their way through. The Hanoverians are 18,000 strong with 54 guns. Falckenstein has collected about 40,000 men behind them; I have done everything to bring together something in front of them, am meeting with great difficulty, but hope to-morrow to be so strong that we can prescribe any conditions. Then the King will have conquered North Germany in eight days. Saxony we may easily lose in the next few days, but no matter, the decision lies in Bohemia. I do not intend to let a Saxon-Bavarian invasion of Saxony disturb me; as soon as ever we are finished with the Hanoverians, the Bavarians shall have enough to do at home. God be with you.

(Prince Frederick Charles in a telegram expressed his apprehension that his army without the I Army Corps—especially as the Elbe Army was not yet near enough—would be too weak to meet the Austrian forces assembling in Bohemia. Moltke at once replied):—

No. 140.
To Stülpnagel.

Berlin, June 23rd.

In reply to the telegram of 7 p.m. this evening, please to submit to His Royal Highness my respectful opinion:

The I Corps has been assigned by His Majesty to the 2nd Army.

The possibility of a direct reinforcement of the left wing of the 1st Army was considered for the case of the main Austrian force being assembled as far forward as behind Reichenberg. This now seems to be by no means the case, and not merely the I Corps but the whole 2nd Army is advancing towards Arnau, so that it will draw upon itself a considerable part, I am afraid even too great a part, of the enemy's forces.

Only a vigorous advance of the 1st Army can disengage the 2nd. If unfortunately the Prince must wait two days for General v. Herwarth still, in that time the I Corps would not get even as far as Hirschberg.

The Austrians are in full march towards the north. The point is to reach the Iser before them. 100,000 men with Prince Frederick Charles at their head and a reserve of 50,000 men a march behind them, have the greatest chances of victory.

(On the evening of June 27th, the 1st Army in its advance into Bohemia had reached the line of the Iser with its troops stretching as far back as Reichenberg. With a view to secure its communications Moltke wrote):—

No. 141.
To the Ministry of War.
Berlin, June 28th.

A request for commandants of communications and of garrisons at the stations of Löbau, Zittau, and Reichenberg.

(The difficulties of the 2nd Army on its march into Bohemia occasioned the following four telegrams):—

No. 142.
To 1st Army. Castle Sichrow.
Telegram.
Berlin, June 28th, 1 p.m.

According to reports received the V Army Corps had yesterday victorious actions at Nachod and Skalitz against Corps Ramming, while the I Army Corps after initial successes at Trautenau has had to retreat in presence of superior forces, apparently Corps Gablenz.

The I Corps will to-day rest and to-morrow resume offensive. The last report from the Guard Corps states that it was on the 26th at Politz. The complete débouchement of the 2nd Army will be materially facilitated by the advance of the 1st Army.

No. 143.
To Stülpnagel.
Telegram.
Berlin, June 29th, 6.35 a.m.

The 2nd Army pushed forward yesterday to Arnau, Königinhof, Skalitz, General Steinmetz fighting two bloody battles to reach Skalitz.

The Crown Prince with only three corps has the mountain defiles behind him, the X, IV, VI, and VIII Austrian Corps before him, the II on his left flank. It seems to me absolutely necessary that he should be disengaged by the 1st Army, which, five corps strong, has against it only the I and III Austrian and the Saxon Corps.

The opportunity of making the most of so great a superiority will perhaps not recur. Should a part of the enemy retreat eccentrically towards Prague, the 1st Army is strong enough to let Herwarth pursue in that direction.

Have insufficient knowledge of your situation, pray reply.

No. 144.

To Prince Frederick Charles.

Telegram.

Berlin, June 29th, 7.30 a.m.

His Majesty expects that the 1st Army by a quickened advance will disengage the 2nd Army, which, in spite of a series of victorious actions, is still for the moment in a difficult situation.

No. 145.

To Blumenthal at Headquarters of 2nd Army viâ *Reinerz.*

Telegram.

Berlin, June 29th, 8.24 p.m.

Certainly the 1st Army must come on; to-day twice ordered. If the enemy's main force is concentrated behind the Elbe, between Josephstadt and Pardubitz, the 2nd Army stands better where it is now than at Gitschin.

Have insufficient knowledge of your situation. Can you live there a few days? Can you support V Corps sufficiently? Where is I Corps?

(On the morning of June 30th the King with the Great Headquarters travelled to Bohemia. Just before he left Berlin came a telegram reporting that the 2nd Army had occupied the line of the Upper Elbe. In consequence of this report the following order was issued during the railway journey):—

No. 146.

To the Commanders of the 1st and 2nd Armies.

Telegram.

Kohlfurt, June 30th, 12.45 p.m.

The 2nd Army has to maintain itself on the left bank of the Upper Elbe, its right wing ready to join on through Königinhof to the left wing of the advancing 1st Army.

The 1st Army is to advance in the direction of Koniggrätz without stopping. Any considerable bodies of the enemy on the right flank of this advance, General Herwarth must attack and drive off from the enemy's main body.

(On June 30th the Great Headquarters reached Reichenberg Next morning, July 1st, was sent off):—

No. 147.

For Publication, Announcing Victory of Gitschin.

Telegram.

(The Great Headquarters moved in the morning of July 1st to Castle Sichrow. Here came a telegram from the Crown Prince reporting that the I Army Corps was to cross the Elbe, and march forward to Miletin, and the rest of the army to follow on July 2nd. As this was contrary to the orders given the day before (No. 146), Moltke sent the following inquiry) :—

No. 148.

To Commander of 2nd Army, Liebau.

Telegram.

Castle Sichrow, July 1st, 1.45 p.m.

According to yesterday's cypher telegram 2nd Army had to maintain itself on the left bank of the Upper Elbe. Had that telegram not yet been received or what reasons led to the decision to go with the whole army on to the right bank ?

No. 149.

To Blumenthal.

Telegram.

Castle Sichrow, July 1st, 4.20 p.m.

I am going this evening to Gitschin. 1st Army rests to-morrow, perhaps also next day. A talk with one of your officers desirable.

(Moltke went to Gitschin on July 1st. The King and Headquarters on July 2nd.)

No. 150.

To Lieutenant-General v. d. Mülbe, Dresden.

Gitschin, July 2nd.

Ordering a reconnaissance towards Theresienstadt with a view to preparing to make use of the railway from Dresden to Prague.

No. 151.*

To the 1st and 2nd Armies.

Gitschin, July 2nd.

The all-important point for the next operations is to get to know the position at this moment of the enemy's main force, as in spite of a series of fortunate actions touch with the enemy has been lost.

It is further necessary to know the conditions in which an attack upon him can be made. Accordingly the following orders are given in the first instance only for July 3rd :—

General v. Herwarth is to be directed upon Chlumetz in order to observe towards Prague and to secure the crossings of the Elbe from Pardubitz downwards. The other corps of the 1st Army will move to the line Neubidschow—Horitz, but a detachment of the left wing is to go towards Sadowa to reconnoitre the line of the Elbe from Koniggrätz to Josephstadt.

If considerable forces of the enemy are still found in front of this line they must be at once attacked with the largest possible superiority of force.

The I Army Corps is to move forwards by Miletin towards Bürglitz, and Cerekwitz to observe towards Josephstadt and must cover the 2nd Army during its march off towards the right, if that march should be ordered. The other corps of the 2nd Army are to remain on July 3rd on the left bank of the Elbe and reconnaissances must be made towards the Aupa and Mettau.

The reports upon ground and upon the whereabouts of the enemy are to be sent here at once. If it should prove from them that a concentric attack of both armies upon the enemy's main force, presumed to be between Josephstadt and Königgrätz would meet with too great difficulties, or that the Austrian army has already left that district, then the whole army will continue its march in the direction of Pardubitz.

The 2nd Army must immediately consider how to secure its supplies during this march.

The Commanders of both armies must send officers to receive orders every evening to the headquarters of His Majesty the King.

---

* See plan 4.

No. 152.
To the 2nd Army, Königinhof.
Gitschin, July 2nd, 11 p.m.

According to reports received by the 1st Army the enemy in about the strength of three corps, which, however, may be still further reinforced, has advanced to and beyond the line formed by the Bistritz at Sadowa and an encounter there with the 1st Army is to be expected very early to-morrow morning. The 1st Army, according to orders, will be to-morrow morning, July 3rd at 2 a.m., with two divisions at Horitz, with one at Milowitz, with one at Cerekwitz, two at Pschanek and Briskan, the Cavalry Corps at Gutwasser.

Your Royal Highness will be good enough immediately to make the necessary arrangements to be able to advance with all your forces in support of the 1st Army against the right flank of the enemy's probable advance, and in so doing to come into action as soon as possible. The directions given from here this afternoon in other conditions (151) are now no longer valid.

No. 153.
To General v. Bonin, Ober-Prausnitz.
Gitschin, July 2nd, 12 p.m.

As far as can be foreseen the 1st Army will be engaged very early to-morrow morning with three corps of the enemy in the neighbourhood of Sadowa on the Bistritz (on the road between Königgrätz and Horitz). Your Excellency will be good enough at once to assemble your corps in order to be quite ready when the orders of His Royal Highness the Crown Prince reach you, or, if need be, to come into action independently.

(During the battle of Königgrätz on July 3rd, Moltke issued only the following order written with pencil on a small card):—

No. 154.
To General of Infantry Herwarth v. Bittenfeldt.
At Sadowa, July 3rd, 1.45 p.m.

Crown Prince at Ziselowes. Retreat of Austrians to Josephstadt cut off. It is of the greatest importance that the corps of General v. Herwarth should advance on the opposite wing while the Austrians are still holding their ground in the centre.

(On the evening of July 3rd, after the battle, the following order was issued) :—

No. 155.
To the Commanders of the 1st and 2nd Armies.
Near Königgrätz, July 3rd, 1866, 6.30 p.m.

To-morrow will be a day of rest, and only those marches are to be carried out which are needed for the comfort of the troops and their return to the normal order. The outposts towards Josephstadt are to be placed by the 2nd Army, those against Königgrätz by the 1st. Troops of General Herwarth's command are, as far as possible, to pursue the enemy, who has retired mainly in the direction of Pardubitz. The Guard-Landwehr Division is to be directed straight for Chlumetz.

(On July 4th and 5th reports on the battle of Königgrätz were sent off).

No. 156.
To Major-General v. Wolff (Chief of the Central Intelligence Office, Berlin).
Telegram.
Horitz, July 4th, 1866.

Publish the following :

Yesterday morning at 7 a.m. the Prussian Army, under the personal command of His Majesty the King, came upon the Austro-Saxon Army of Feld Zeugmeister *v.* Benedek. The battle which ensued lasted twelve hours, the enemy, maintaining with great stubbornness for six hours a strong position behind the Bistritz. Our columns which reached the battlefield punctually, some of them from a great distance, at last, at 2 p.m., succeeded in taking the enemy's position by storm. From that time on the enemy was quickly driven back from position to position. At 7 p.m. what was left of the beaten army was in full retreat towards the south.

Our victory, won under the eyes of His Majesty the King, is complete, though bought by heavy losses. The enemy's losses are even greater, and he leaves many prisoners, guns, and other trophies in our hands.

No. 157.
To v. Wolff.
Telegram.
Berlin, Horitz, July 5th, 1.50 a.m.

Publish: The following details of our army's brilliant victory in the battle of Königgrätz, upon July 3rd, are officially known.

We have taken 18,000 to 20,000 prisoners, 120 guns and three colours. Numbers of further prisoners are still being brought in. The enemy's whole army was engaged. We have prisoners of all his corps. General v. Benedek, who had himself intended to attack on that day, commanded in person. When about 2 p.m. his position behind the Bistritz had been stormed and the Austro-Saxon army began its retreat, His Majesty the King placed himself at the head of the pursuing cavalry.

(After the army had rested on July 4th, it was to advance on the 5th to the Elbe, and at the same time to pursue the retreating enemy with an advance guard. For this purpose the following orders were issued):—

No. 158.
To the Minister of War, General v. Roon.
Horitz, July 4th, 1866.

I respectfully inform Your Excellency that His Majesty the King has to-day released General v. Herwarth from his connection with the 1st Army, and placed him under His Own direct command.

(Herwarth's command is hereafter described by the title of "Elbe Army.")

No. 159.
To the Commanders of the 1st, 2nd and Elbe Armies.
Horitz, July 4th, 1866.

In consideration of the uncommonly rapid course of the operations so far it is His Majesty's intention to give the troops a rest.

First, however, the armies are to be collected, the 1st about Pardubitz—Chrudim, the 2nd in rear of the line Bjela—Prschelautsch. Herwarth's army which once more comes under the direct command of His Majesty, is to march to Chlumetz, its Guard-Landwehr Division to Podiebrad, and to protect itself in the direction of Prague.

The 1st Army has to pursue the enemy's retreat by an advance guard, to be sufficiently provided with cavalry, and in particular to reconnoitre the region towards Leitomischl. It will depend upon the information obtained by this advance guard whether, and to what extent, the 2nd Army and that of General v. Herwarth can be billeted.

For the march ordered above towards the Elbe, the 1st Army is to use the road leading along this river to Pardubitz, the 2nd Army that through Bohdanetsch to Prschelautsch, which latter will form the limit between the billets of the two armies. The 2nd Army has itself to protect the transport of its supplies, so long as they come from Silesia, against Josephstadt and Königgrätz. This headquarters will do all it can to have the railway line Löbau—Jung Bunzlau put into working order as soon as possible. The 1st Army must itself protect this, its communication with the rear, by suitable guards from stage to stage, until the arrival of the necessary unmobilized troops which have been requisitioned from Prussia.

(This order was modified on the same day as follows) :—

No. 160.

Horitz, July 4th, 8.30 p.m.

In consequence of reports which have only this moment been received, especially of the changed position of the 1st Army, it is determined that in order to avoid crossings :—

The 2nd Army is to advance to Pardubitz, to reconnoitre towards Leitomischl, and protect towards Königgrätz and Josephstadt the communications with Silesia. The 1st Army is to go to Prschelautsch and protect its communications with Turnau by suitable garrisons of the principal points on the route. With regard to the Elbe Army, there is no change of the order issued to-day at noon. Finally the concession is made that two days may be devoted to the march ordered to the Elbe.

(In order to have the railway Löbau—Jung Bunzlau set in working order as promised in No. 159, Moltke addressed himself to the Minister of War) :—

No. 161.
To Roon.

Horitz, July 4th.

As an Intendant has not been appointed for the whole army I respectively request Your Excellency to be good enough to communicate with the Ministry of Trade on the subject of bringing into working order the railway line Löbau—Turnau—Jung Bunzlau (later on, if required, as far as Prague), which is absolutely necessary for the supply of provisions to the army. For this purpose it will be necessary to supply a sufficient number of railway officials of all classes. The interests of the army might in the present case justify even such a reduction of traffic as this would produce on the home lines.

I also request Your Excellency to place at our disposal the Landwehr Infantry from those fortresses which, in consequence of the favourable progress of our operations, seem to be no longer threatened, in numbers sufficient to protect the communications of the army, in particular the railway stations Löbau, Zittau, Reichenberg, Turnau, Münchengrätz, Jung Bunzlau, which are the end-points of stages on the lines of communications, and to forward these troops to the main points, which until then will be occupied by the army. These detachments are to be charged not only with the protection of the stations but also with that of the lines and telegraphs, for which they are to supply suitable patrols.

Be so kind as to communicate to me the arrangements you make.

(For the restoration and protection of railway communications with the rear and for the establishment of regular requisitions, Moltke issued following orders on July 5th):—

No. 162.
To Lt.-Gen. v. d. Mülbe, Dresden.

Telegram.

Horitz, July 5th.

Inquires how No. 150 has been carried out. Informs him that Guard-Landwehr Division is this day reaching Podiebrad, and that it is intended to send the reserve corps to Prague. Mülbe to send reports daily, especially information about the enemy.

No. 163.

To the Commanders of the 1st and 2nd Armies.

Horitz, July 5th.

2nd Army to repair the line Pardubitz—Prague, and to reconnoitre the line through Josephstadt and Königgrätz to Pardubitz, in order to ascertain whether temporary lines can be laid to pass round the two fortresses and in that way railway communication with Reichenberg be established.

The troops of the reserve corps from Dresden will set in order the railway from that place to Prague.

No. 164.

To the Commander of the Elbe Army.

Horitz, July 5th.

Guard-Landwehr Division to be sent in two marches from Podiebrad to Prague, which it is to occupy. It will probably be strong enough for the purpose, but the Elbe Army must support it by a second division to keep about a day's march behind. Elbe Army also to secure crossings of Elbe at Elbeteinitz and Kolin, to protect the railway at those places, and seize any engines and carriages there.

2nd Army's railway troops to restore railway Pardubitz—Prague. Mülbe been ordered to attend to railway Dresden—Prague.

Connection between the two divisions of the reserve corps should be restored.

No. 165.

To Commanders of 1st, 2nd and Elbe Armies.

Horitz, July 5th.

The rapid advance of the operations and the inadequacy of the Turnau Railway to bring up supplies for the whole army make it absolutely necessary to obtain what is wanted, or at least a good part of it, by requisitions. To avoid loss of time the requisitions must not be made by the Intendants, but in the interests of discipline and to prevent waste, they must not degenerate into the men helping themselves.

Each of the three armies must assign the villages within its rayon to its army corps; these to their division and so downwards, in such fashion that every unit (battalion, regiment, brigade) has given to it a particular village, where the requisitions are to be carried out under the conduct of officers, so that the provisions may reach the hands of the troops as soon as possible. The armies and the army corps are to issue the most stringent orders against self-help or plunder, and those who contravene them are to be treated with all the strictness of military law.

Even though some villages will be temporarily deserted by their inhabitants there will always be found in them supplies to cover some of the needs. The troops are to be instructed to drive with them cattle, which may be found, if not in the villages, at any rate in the woods. In any places where more than enough for the needs of the day is found it must be used to replace the iron ration.

(On July 6th the deployment of the army on the line Pardubitz—Chlumetz was completed. Thereupon the advance towards Moravia was to begin. For this the following orders were issued on July 6th and 7th):—

No. 166.

To the Commander of the Elbe Army.

Horitz, July 6th.

From the report of the Chief of Staff of the Elbe Army of the 5th instant, I have gathered that army's intended movements during the next few days. They call for the following observations: now that the deployment of the three armies on the line Pardubitz-Chlumetz has been carried out, the general operations are to be continued towards the south-east, and have already been begun by the 2nd Army, which is advancing to-day from Pardubitz towards Hohenmauth. It is therefore desirable that the division intended to support the Guard-Landwehr should not be sent further towards the west than the circumstances absolutely require, in order that hereafter, when the Guard-Landwehr is left at Prague, the supporting division may be able as soon as possible to rejoin the Elbe Army in its movements towards the south-east. Headquarters of His Majesty the King move to-day to Pardubitz.

No. 167.

To the Commanders of the 1st, 2nd and Elbe Armies.

Pardubitz, July 6th, 8.45 p.m.

The advance towards Moravia will begin to-morrow. The 2nd Army, except the VI Corps, is to follow the enemy in the direction of Mährisch-Trübau. The 1st Army is to march by Chrudim—Skutsch in the direction of Politschka. The Elbe Army by Tschaslau and Kreutzberg. Although this advance is practically protected by the 2nd Army yet the other two armies must form their own advance guards, but may then, to save the troops, and to make the most of the resources of the country, march on a broad front and make use of the minor roads. The position of armies, corps and divisions is to be reported daily.

Until further notice officers are to be sent to Pardubitz to fetch the orders from the Headquarters of His Majesty.

A summary return of the marching strength of each battalion, cavalry regiment and battery is to be sent in by the 10th instant.

No. 168.

To the Commanders of the 1st, 2nd and Elbe Armies.

Pardubitz, July 7th, 9 a.m.

The quick advance of the army prevents the regular service of supplies from keeping pace with it. As, moreover, the condition of the enemy admits of a larger interval between the marching columns, the Elbe Army from this time on is given the direction from Tschaslau through Deutschbrod upon Iglau so that the two great roads from Chrudim by Skutsch and Politschka, as well as by Kreutzberg and Neustadtl fall to the 1st Army. With a view to the support, which may possibly become necessary in the improbable case of the enemy's attack from the direction of Olmütz, the Second Army must keep up constant communication with the left wing column of the First Army. So long as the rearward communications of the 2nd Army pass through Königinhof, and so long as the clearing up of the battlefield of Königgrätz makes it needful, the VI Army Corps must remain substantially in its present position, and must also protect Pardubitz by a detachment. Afterwards this corps too must be brought up through Pardubitz to the 2nd Army, which during its further advance must arrange to base its communications through Mittelwalde on the County of

Glatz. But until the Landwehr troops, which have been called for to occupy the important railway line Pardubitz—Prague, have arrived, the VI Army Corps, even when it advances, will provide a detachment to hold Pardubitz. In order to avoid detailed orders from here no attempt is made to lay down a strict limit between the billets of the three armies marching side by side.

But it is laid down as the principle by which to decide any possible conflict of claims that the two wing armies must always spread their billets towards the outer flank in order to compress as little as possible the district in which the centre army can be billeted.

(In explanation of the above orders Moltke wrote on July 8th the following letter):—

No. 169.

To the Commanders of the 1st, 2nd and Elbe Armies.

Pardubitz, July 8th, 9 p.m.

By His Majesty's command I communicate below to the Commanders of armies the intentions upon which the operations now beginning are based, of which, however, only so much as is necessary for the attainment of the purpose is to be made known to the officers commanding under their orders.

To the 2nd Army is given the mission of posting itself over against Olmütz upon the line Littau—Konitz, and its advance guard will constantly seek to reach the enemy and to gather the most accurate possible news of the whereabouts of his main body. A formal attack upon Olmütz is not intended, though the 2nd Army will use every opportunity for possible surprises and try to prevent the enemy from quietly recovering condition. In the improbable case of a general offensive of the army from Olmütz with decidedly superior forces the 2nd Army would have to retire not upon the two others but upon the County of Glatz, and to draw the enemy after it. Accordingly the rearward communications of this army are to be based upon Glatz.

The 1st Army is to make for Brünn along the two roads by Politschka—Kunstadt, and by Kreutzberg—Roschinka.

The Elbe Army from Iglau on will be given its further direction according to how things stand with the enemy, either likewise upon Brünn or through Znaim. At Iglau it must forthwith proceed to lay down a great magazine. His Majesty's Headquarters are to move on the 9th to Hohenmauth, where, therefore, a suitable detachment for its protection must be left behind by the 2nd Army, and on the 10th to Zwittau.

Reports of the Elbe Army are, during the next few days, to be forwarded by the 1st Army, and for this purpose these armies must communicate to one another the arrangements for their respective marches. Any decision concerning the strengthening or weakening of the army posted against Ölmütz or that operating towards Vienna, is reserved. Meanwhile the assembly of the whole of the I Reserve Corps at Prague is already proceeding.

(In continuation of the order of July 5th, on the subject of requisitions (No. 165), and of a royal order in Cabinet on July 8th, dealing with the same subject, Moltke for the purpose of establishing order behind the army issued the following instruction):—

No. 170.

To the Commanders of the 1st, 2nd and Elbe Armies.

Pardubitz, July 8th.

1. Military police to keep to their duty of superintending traffic.
2. Officers to obey the instructions of the military police.
3. Wagon trains not to be prolonged by the admission of needless vehicles.
4. Traffic at defiles to be controlled by senior officers. Foddering on the road to be prohibited.
5. Convoys, in future, to have escorts strong enough to protect them against probable cavalry attacks.
6. Railways and telegraphs never to be damaged without orders. Rather to be protected and repaired for future use.

(On July 8th the Austrian Lieut.-Field-Marshal Baron v. Gablenz appeared at the great Headquarters at Pardubitz, bringing proposals for the conclusion of an armistice which was to extend not only to the theatre of war in Bohemia, but also to that in South Germany. The conditions suggested were, however, not such as Prussia could accept, the less so in that meanwhile Austria had ceded Venetia to France and therefore there was a danger that an armistice might be used by Austria to bring over to the northern theatre of war the troops thus set free in Italy. General v. Gablenz was, therefore, not received by the King, but instead General v. Moltke in person handed to him the following written decision):—

No. 171.

To the Imperial Royal Lieut.-Field-Marshal Baron v. Gablenz.

Pardubitz, July 8th.

Your Excellency has permitted me to see your instructions for the conclusion of an armistice, and I have not failed to report their substance to His Majesty the King.

His Majesty would be very ready to consent to a truce for the purpose of negotiations which might lead to a lasting peace between Prussia and Austria. Overtures forming a political basis for such negotiations have, however, not been made to us, and, moreover, our relations with Italy require an understanding with that Power before we can come to a definite decision.

But His Majesty would not now in any circumstances be in a position to accept conditions of an armistice such as are contained in Your Excellency's instructions.

(In the days from July 9th to 11th the Prussian army continued its advance to Vienna while observing Olmütz, whither the greater part of the Austrian Northern Army, under General Benedek, had retired, and on the last-named day reached the line of the Thaya with the advance guard of the Elbe Army. During this advance Moltke issued the following orders):—

No. 172.

To the Commander of the Elbe Army, Deutschbrod.

Hohenmauth, July 9th.

The Elbe Army is to send off at once from Iglau towards Znaim a division, to be reinforced as strongly as possible with cavalry, as advance guard of the Prussian Army advancing towards Vienna. This division has to keep connection, as well as it can, with the remainder of the Elbe Army, marching on the two roads by Trebisch and Grosmeseritsh towards Brünn. All reports of the division are to be communicated to me.

No. 173.

To Lt.-Gen. v. d. Mülbe, Dresden.

Telegram.

Zwittau, July 11th, 9.51 a.m.

Inform Commandant of Königstein by flag of truce that any damage done by fortress to railway will occasion Prussian reprisals in Saxony, *e.g.*, wholesale seizure of carts to take the place of the railway. If railway damaged, execute this measure. Same procedure at Theresienstadt during your advance. If line blocked, say at Lobositz, must do your best to clear it.

No. 174.

To the Commanders of the 1st, 2nd and Elbe Armies.

Zwittau, July 11th, 11 a.m.

His Majesty's Headquarters move to-morrow, the 12th, to Tschernahora. To protect the headquarters the 8th Division will occupy a district bounded towards the east by the villages Zwittawka—Boskowitz, Petrowitz and Blansko, one battalion at Tschernahora.

The first infantry brigade will to-morrow morning so arrange its march towards Gewitsch as to occupy Brüsau till His Majesty has passed this place and will reconnoitre in advance towards Lettowitz and Gewitsch. The brigade will then be recalled to the I Army Corps. According to the information received through the 2nd Army, and yesterday evening communicated from here to the 1st and Elbe Armies, the enemy is likely to have at Brünn nothing more than the 10th Austrian Army Corps, which retired in that direction, a part of the cavalry and whatever reinforcements it has been practicable meanwhile to bring up from Vienna. The Commander of the 1st Army will judge on the spot to what extent in these circumstances any concentration of his army towards Brünn is required to obtain possession of that place, or whether it would not rather be now safe for the 1st Army also to use the road through Eibenschütz in order to facilitate and expedite the deployment of the 1st and Elbe Armies behind the Thaya on the line Znaim—Muschau. On the basis of the information on this subject which must be directly communicated by the 1st Army to the Elbe Army, the Elbe Army must either continue its march towards Brünn through Stannern and Trebitsch (or if required Grossmeseritsch), or if a concentration at Brünn should prove needless, must advance with all its forces directly upon Znaim, So soon as this point has been decided on the spot the decision must be reported.

No. 175.

To the Commander of the 2nd Army, Mährisch—Trübau.

Zwittau, July 11th.

In the order dated Pardubitz, July 8th (169), the line Littau—Konitz was assigned to the 2nd Army for its position over against Olmütz, and this army was instructed to base itself upon Glatz. But in view of the inner superiority of this army over the enemy, who has retired to Olmütz and of the enemy's condition, which is every day revealing itself more clearly, it can now no longer be considered dangerous for the 2nd Army to spread itself towards the south and south-east for the more perfect observation of the enemy, making a special point of interrupting the communication between Olmütz and Vienna by the railway, and of discovering in time, and preventing, either the reinforcement or the departure of the enemy by this railway line.

No. 176.

To the Commander of the 1st Army, Brünn.

Brünn, July 13th.

His Majesty grants the troops of the 1st Army a two days' rest after their exhausting marches.

The commander of the army will at once bring up by road to Pardubitz the two pontoon columns which were earlier ordered to Turnau. They are to be kept ready at Pardubitz to be moved on by railway, if and when hereafter ordered. The suggestion that fifty heavy guns should be brought up need not at present be carried out. A decision on this point is reserved.

No. 177.

To the Commander of the 2nd Army, Opatowitz.

Brünn, July 13th.

The previous orders are in general confirmed, according to which the 2nd Army, basing itself upon the County of Glatz, has to prevent the enemy, who has retired to Olmütz, from restoring his condition, as well as to prevent movements of the enemy to and fro between Vienna and Olmütz. The second of these tasks can be best fulfilled by the nearer approach of the 2nd Army to the fortress of Olmütz, and by the interruption of the railway line at some suitable point attainable by the army between Prerau and Lundenburg.

For the transmission of orders from the King's headquarters to the 2nd Army it is desirable that the field telegraph should connect itself at the nearest suitable point with the Zwittau—Brünn railway. Assuming this to be done the daily despatch of officers for the same purpose may be suspended in view of the now considerably greater distance.

The 2nd Army, however, will be so good as to report always, without delay, by the telegraph line to be thus established, all reports about the enemy's movements at Olmütz which may be of importance for the further operations of the whole army.

Postal communications through Glatz are to be established by the 2nd Army as soon as possible.

No. 178.
To General Herwarth v. Bittenfeldt.

Brünn, July 13th.

As the 1st Army yesterday occupied Brünn without fighting, and a concentration of a large force here has, therefore, become needless, the order already issued with a view to that eventuality, which, however, seems not to have reached Your Excellency, is hereby repeated and in accordance with it the whole Elbe Army is now to advance directly upon Znaim.

Your Excellency will be good enough at once to modify, in accordance with the above order, the arrangements reported to me in the letter of Colonel v. Schlotheim, dated Trebitsch, July 12th, 2 p.m., for the marching of the Elbe Army in the direction of Lundenburg.

No. 179.
To Major-General v. Wolff.
Telegram.

Brünn, July 13th.

Account, for publication, of King's entry into Brünn.

(As the Austrian Army in Olmütz did nothing, and as an attack upon it in its entrenched camp offered little prospect of success, it became clear that a decision of the campaign could be brought about only by a further advance towards Vienna. In this movement it was important quickly to cross the space between the Thaya and the Danube, and to have ready the means of crossing the Danube. With this object Moltke, on July 14th, issued the following orders) :—

No. 180.

To the Commanders of the 1st, 2nd and Elbe Armies, and to the Guard-Landwehr Division.*

Brünn, July 14th.

After the expiry of the two days' rest granted by His Majesty to the troops of the 1st Army this army is to set out on the further advance across the Thaya towards Vienna, for which purpose it may make use of the roads—

(*a*) Eibenschütz—Laa—Ernstbrunn.
(*b*) Dürnholz—Ladendorf.
(*c*) Muschau—Nikolsburg—Gaunersdorf.

In addition a detachment, of which the strength is to be decided by the Commander of the I Army Corps, is to move on Lundenburg. Its advance guard, to be pushed far in front, has as soon as possible to make the railway to Prerau impracticable for the enemy; but the railway Brünn—Lundenburg—Gänserndorf is to be preserved for our use, and therefore to be occupied as the enemy advances and any damage to it to be prevented.

The Elbe army, which by an order of yesterday's date (No. 178) was directed upon Znaim, is to march from there by the two roads—

(*a*) Jetzelsdorf—Oberhollabrunn,
(*b*) Joslowitz—Enzersdorf-im-Thal,

and will also send off a detachment to Maissau, in order later from here to demonstrate against the Upper Danube between Tulln and Krems.

In order during these movements of the 1st and Elbe Armies to secure, in case of need, their mutual support, it is appointed that the Thaya must be crossed at Muschau and at Znaim by the two main bodies on the 17th instant.

The 1st Army will be set in march through Pardubitz along the Brünn railway to Brünn, its two pontoon columns which

---

* The Guard Landwehr Infantry Division (Major-General v. Rosenberg), the combined Landwehr Infantry Division (Major-General v. Bentheim), the combined Landwehr Cavalry Division (Major-General Count zu Dohna), and the Reserve Field Regiment (Colonel v. Zimmermann) formed together the I Reserve Corps.

were previously directed to Turnau (No. 176); the 2nd Army also, will at once march off all its pontoon columns to Brünn. The march tables for the pontoon columns are to be sent to me as soon as possible by the commanders of the two armies, so that arrangements may be made for their further transport by railway.

The Guard Landwehr Division v. Rosenberg will set out on the 16th instant for Pardubitz, temporarily leaving a detachment at Prague. Those concerned are hereby informed that it is intended, after the arrival of the Division v. Bentheim at Prague, to bring up this division together with the detachment of the Division Rosenberg left there in garrison, by railway from Prague, and the Division Rosenberg by railway from Pardubitz to the main army; the Division Bentheim, however, will have to leave at Prague an infantry brigade, a cavalry regiment and a battery. The details of these movements by railway cannot be settled until the railway from Prague to Brünn has been put into working order.

The headquarters of His Majesty the King remain until further notice at Brünn, which is to be occupied by a detachment of the I Army Corps. All three armies will at once post letter parties between their headquarters and Brünn. By these letter parties all the latest events and the intentions of the commanders for the next day are every day to be reported here. The 1st Army will also have to take special measures to secure its line of supplies from Brünn.

No. 181.

To the Commanders of the 1st and Elbe Armies.

Brünn, July 14th.

In the order issued to-day from here (No. 180) concerning the further advance, the armies were instructed to cross the Thaya on the 17th instant. But as according to the dispositions which have meanwhile been received both armies reach the Thaya on the 15th instant there is no objection to this river being crossed before the 17th.

(In the night of July 14th to 15th, the Great Headquarters received from the 2nd Army a report that the greater part of the Austrian forces had moved off from Olmütz and were marching towards Prerau. This caused the following modifications of the orders issued on July 14th):—

No. 182.

To the Commander of the 1st Army, Prödlitz.

Brünn, July 15th, 8 a.m.

According to the report from your office of yesterday's date, it is to be assumed that the enemy's army has left Olmütz in the direction of Prerau. The 1st Army at Brünn does not need support by the 2nd, of which the task still is to watch Olmütz and to delay, as long as possible, the further departure of the enemy.

Your Royal Highness will, therefore, bring up the Guard and VI Corps by the shortest way to Olmütz, but set in march in the direction of Kremsier and Napagedl the corps which are to-day moving towards Prossnitz, which must again get touch with the enemy.

In consequence of these new circumstances the 1st and the Elbe Armies, which stand to-day at the Thaya, must for the time give up the march on which they have already started towards Vienna.

To-morrow, the 16th, the Elbe Army will advance beyond Laa in order to reconnoitre towards Vienna, and to oppose a possible advance of the enemy from that place. The 1st Army, of which the 8th Division will to-day reach Göding, will to-morrow, the 16th, concentrate round Lundenburg and attack the army retreating from Olmütz, if it should attempt to retreat towards Vienna or even towards Pressburg.

Those corps of the 2nd Army which have been directed upon Kremsier and Napagedl must operate as though they were a strong advance guard pushed forward by the 1st Army, with which they must keep themselves in communication, and by which, if necessary, they will be supported.

Arrangements going beyond the 16th cannot be made with certainty till the Commander of the 1st Army has ascertained on the spot whether the whole army, or only parts of it, have left Olmütz, but it is now important to observe that the railway line Oderberg—Weisskirchen—Lundenburg may become of great importance for our own use, and that it is, therefore, not to be destroyed but to be protected as well as possible from enterprises from Olmütz, especially at Prerau, and where it has been interrupted is to be immediately restored. The orders that it may be necessary to send for this purpose to Upper Silesia, His Royal Highness the Commander of the 1st Army, will be good enough to issue.

No. 183.

To the Commander of the Elbe Army, Znaim.

Brünn, July 15th, 8 a.m.

According to a report received during the night from the 2nd Army, the enemy has moved off from Olmütz and, in whole or in part, is marching upon Prerau.

Accordingly, the 2nd Army has been instructed to set in march the I and V Army Corps from Prossnitz to Kremsier and Napagedl; further, instructions have been sent to the 1st Army to concentrate to-morrow, the 16th, towards Lundenburg, in order to block the enemy's retreat towards Vienna or towards Pressburg, and eventually to attack him with five army corps.

To protect this operation against possible enterprises from Vienna the Commander of the Elbe Army will now direct his forces from Znaim through Laa towards Wilfersdorf, and reconnoitre in the direction of Vienna. In case considerable forces should move forward from Vienna, the Elbe Army would have to fall back on the 1st Army.

The railway through Lundenburg is not to be cut by parties sent out, but rather to be protected, as an advance towards Vienna is still kept in view.

No. 184.

To the Commander of the 1st Army, Brünn.

Brünn, July 15th, 8 a.m.

According to a report received during the night from the 2nd Army the enemy has moved off from Olmütz and, in whole or in part, is marching upon Prerau.

Accordingly the 2nd Army has been instructed to set in march the I and the V Army Corps from Prossnitz to Kremsier and Napagedl. These two corps will operate as a strong advance guard pushed far to the front of the 1st Army, and that army, in the new circumstances, is to march to-morrow morning, the 16th, towards Lundenburg in order to block the enemy's retreat to Vienna or to Pressburg, and eventually to attack him with five army corps.

Further arrangements cannot be made until more definite reports of the strength and direction of the retreating enemy have come in from the 2nd Army.

In order, however, to cover in rear, in any circumstances, the operations of the 1st Army, the Elbe Army has been instructed to march to-morrow, the 16th, to Laa, and afterwards to place itself at Wilfersdorf, upon the road to Vienna. In case the forces of the enemy should advance from Vienna, the Elbe Army will fall back upon the 1st Army, and it will then depend upon the exact circumstances whether with six and a half army corps we shall turn against the Austrian northern or southern army.

At present there is no more to be noted except that the railway Vienna—Lundenburg—Weisskirchen—Oderburg may become of importance for our own use, and is, therefore, not to be interrupted, and that the 2nd Army has been entrusted with its protection, in particular at Prerau, and in case of need with its restoration on the frontier of Upper Silesia.

(In a letter of General Blumenthal, written from Konitz on July 15th, the proposal had been made that after the departure of the Austrians from Olmütz only the I Army Corps should be left in front of this fortress, that the V Army Corps and the Cavalry Division should follow the enemy in the direction of Kremsier, and then along the railway on his flank, crossing the March after him, if necessary. The Guard and VI Army Corps were to reach Brünn on July 17th; General Blumenthal requested an order that they might advance upon the direct road to Vienna. Moltke replied) :—

No. 185.

To the Commander of the 2nd Army, Prödlitz.

Brünn, July 16th, a.m.

From the report of the 2nd Army of the 15th instant, and from the oral explanations of General v. Stosch (Quartermaster-General of the 2nd Army), it appears that in all probability the whole of the Austrian northern army has left Olmütz, and that, therefore, for the observation of that place a weaker fraction of our force than was previously intended will suffice.

His Majesty, therefore, approves of the proposal that only the I Army Corps should now be charged with this duty, especially as it will shortly be reinforced by the Reserve Corps of General v. d. Mülbe.

It also seems appropriate to the circumstances that the further movement of the enemy's army along the March should be flanked by the V Army Corps. Although this corps alone is unable directly to bar the enemy's march, yet it will find opportunity in the manner proposed at the headquarters of the 2nd Army of damaging the enemy by offensive strokes across the river, and in any case of finding out the direction of his retreat.

If this retreat were intended to be towards Vienna or Pressburg its execution would be made impossible by the 1st Army. There is, however, no intention of following the enemy to Komorn or further eastwards, but in that case we should carry out the advance towards Vienna which would be joined by the Guard and VI Corps and the pontoon trains of the 2nd Army.

For the present no other directive instructions can be given from here; we must wait for information of the direction in which the army is retreating from Olmütz.

It is noted for your information that yesterday two trains on the railway to Vienna passed Lundenburg, but a third had to turn back, because the 8th Division had occupied Göding.

(The Austrian northern army under Benedek had retired in forced marches from Olmütz into the Lesser Carpathians, in order from here to reach the Danube at Vienna or Pressburg. It could not be the intention of the Prussian Commander-in-Chief to follow the enemy on this roundabout way, but seemed more advantageous to take the shortest way to the Danube, to cross this river below Vienna and so to separate Benedek's army from the forces assembling at the capital. For this purpose during the next days the following orders were issued):—

No. 186.

*To the Commanders of the 1st, 2nd and Elbe Armies.**

Brünn, July 17th.

The circumstances of the moment render it necessary to regulate from here the movements of the 1st, 2nd and Elbe Armies, and the directive instructions for them can be given for only a short time in advance.

His Majesty's general intention is for an advance towards the Danube, but whether the direction is to be that of Vienna or of Pressburg cannot yet be determined.

The Elbe Army is to follow the great road from Brünn to

---

* This order was sent at 5 p.m. by field couriers to the headquarters of the 1st and Elbe Armies—the headquarters of the 2nd Army was at Brünn—and its substance was also sent by telegram at 8 p.m.

Vienna, observing as it goes the roads on its right flank which lead from Dürnholz and Laa to Vienna.

1st Army will advance upon both banks of the March, protecting or restoring the crossings over this river. This army has to prevent the retreat of forces of the enemy from Olmütz and Vienna to Pressburg. A line just west of Gänserndorf—Zistersdorf will be the demarkation between the Elbe Army and the 1st Army.

The 2nd Army, so far as it can be spared from before Olmütz, will assemble on the line Nikolsburg—Lundenburg and immediately follow the movement of the 1st and Elbe Armies.

The 1st and Elbe Armies are to keep pace with one another during their advance. In order to reach the Danube with concentrated forces the marches are to be made short until the 2nd Army, which to-day reaches Brünn from the neighbourhood of Kremsier, can come up.

As an offensive of the enemy from Vienna, and even from Pressburg also, is by no means impossible, the situation requires that our armies, and especially the Elbe Army, should close up and have strong advance guards. The Elbe Army is to concentrate to-morrow, the 18th, round Wilfersdorf, and to await orders for a general advance.

The 1st Army has to bear in mind that one division may be destined, by a rapid advance from Malacka, to seize Pressburg, the crossing of the Danube at that place, and if possible the points Hainburg and Kittsee. For this movement, however, the order is as yet kept back.

Of what precedes the Royal Commanders are to communicate to the commanders of the troops under their orders only so much as is requisite for the attainment of the object.

From this time on officers are again to be sent every day to these headquarters, and they must be able to give an account of the position of the divisions.

His Majesty's headquarters go to-morrow, the 18th, to Nikolsburg, where a battalion of the 1st Army must, for the present, be left.

The pontoon columns of the 2nd Army, which reach Mödritz and Raigern to-day, will rest there one day and then follow behind the Guard and VI Army Corps; those of the 1st Army which will reach Brünn by road on the 20th, will be instructed to follow.

Brünn is to continue to be occupied by the 2nd Army until the arrival of the Landwehr battalions, which are now on their way. A suitable superior officer is to be appointed by the 2nd Army as permanent commandant of this important point.

The reserve corps of General v. d. Mülbe has its first echelon already on the march from Prague to reinforce the I Army Corps on its way from Olmütz.

(The orders mentioned in this letter to the Guard and VI Army Corps, and to the pontoon columns of the 2nd Army, are not given, as they have the same wording as No. 187.)

No. 187.

To the Commander of the 2nd Army, Brünn.

Brünn, July 18th.

To-morrow, the 19th, the 2nd Army will continue its advance with the Guard and VI Army Corps along the Lundenburg and the Nikolsburg roads, and this has been already notified to both corps.

The V Army Corps is to be sent forward in the direction of Göding or of Skalitz as circumstances may determine. The pontoon columns of the 2nd Army will, to-day, by direct orders from here, be set in march to Auspitz, and will to-morrow reach Köstl, from which point they are to be further directed by the Commander of the 1st Army, under whose orders they come until further notice.

No. 188.

To the Commander of the 1st Army.

Nikolsburg, July 18th, 11 p.m.

The Elbe Army stands with its advance guard at Mistelbach, advance troops in Gaunersdorf, with the 14th Division at Asparn, 16th Division at Wilfersdorf, 15th Division at Wenzersdorf, and must rest to-morrow in this position.

The Guard and VI Army Corps will to-morrow reach at the furthest the line Pawlowitz-Muschau. In these circumstances the advance of the 1st Army ordered for to-morrow must not go beyond the line Malacka—Gaunersdorf, though it is not forbidden to push on parties for special objects, *e.g.*, for the interruption of the telegraph line Vienna—Pressburg. On the whole, however, the army must wait until it is closed up in itself and until the Guard and VI Army Corps come up in second line.

The pontoon columns of the 2nd Army will to-morrow, the 19th, reach Köstl, where they come under the orders of the 1st Army, from which they are to receive the directions for their further march. His Majesty expressly draws attention to the need of precautions against an attack by the enemy from Florisdorf.

No. 189.

To the Commander of the Elbe Army, Florisdorf.

Nikolsburg, July 18th, 11 p.m.

The Elbe Army is to remain until further notice in its present position. The 1st Army has been instructed to come up level with the Elbe Army, and not to pass the line Malacka—Gaunersdorf. His Majesty expressly draws attention to the need of precautions against an attack by the enemy from Florisdorf.

(The nearer the Prussian army approached the Austrian capital the greater became the probability, contemplated by General v. Moltke in the concluding sentence of the last letter, of an Austrian attack from the position of Florisdorf.

Moltke, therefore, first of all worked out the following short draft, written in pencil) :—

No. 190.

Without date, apparently July 18th.

If the enemy starts from Florisdorf on the offensive on July 20th:

> July 20th—If the enemy this day attacks Gaunersdorf General Herwarth in the evening will have to hold his ground at Gaunersdorf.
> Prince Frederick Charles will concentrate to his right and move against the right flank of the attack.
> If the superiority is too great—road to Wilfersdorf to be cleared.
> July 21st.—Rear guard division at Gaunersdorf.
> Retreat of Herwarth before dawn to Wilfersdorf, where half VI Army Corps in support.
> Prince Frederick Charles by Spannberg to Zistersdorf.
> From Malacka whatever is available to Hohenau; Guard Corps to Böhmischkrut.

If by July 20th there has not yet been a general offensive:

July 21st.—VI Army Corps: Wilfersdorf—Mistelbach.
Guard Corps: Böhmischkrut—Wilfersdorf.
July 22nd—Headquarters: Wilfersdorf or Zistersdorf.
Herwarth: Wilfersdorf.
Prince Frederick Charles: Dürnkrut.
Crown Prince: Eisgrub.

(In order to bring up against Vienna as an additional force the available portions of the I Reserve Corps under General v. d. Mülbe the following orders were issued):—

No. 191.
To the Commandant of Brünn.
Telegram.

Nikolsburg, July 19th.

The following order is to be communicated to General v. Rosenberg, Commander of the Guard-Landwehr division, who will arrive in Brünn to-morrow by railway:

The troops of the Guard-Landwehr division arriving in Brünn are at once to march in echelons along the Vienna road to Wilfersdorf. Stages, say, first to Pohrlitz and second to Nikolsburg. The troops may be billeted. From Wilfersdorf onwards instructions for the further march will be given by the Elbe Army. As soon as the railway line to Lundenburg can be opened to traffic the railway journey must be continued as far as Lundenburg, from which place Wilfersdorf can be reached in one march. The Commandant of Brünn has accordingly to communicate to the first echelon of the division, which arrives at Brünn this evening, His Majesty's order to march to-morrow to Pohrlitz.

No. 192.
To Lieut.-General v. d. Mülbe, Prague.

Nikolsburg, July 19th.

General Rosenberg has been instructed from here to join the Elbe Army by marching in echelons to Wilfersdorf (road Brünn—Vienna) with the troops of the Guard Landwehr Division, which are to be sent by the railway to Brünn (afterwards perhaps to Lundenburg). Your Excellency will cause the troops of the Division Bentheim, so far as they are not required by previous orders to remain to garrison Prague, immediately to follow the railway transport and march of the Guard Landwehr Division.

No. 193.
To the Commander of the Elbe Army.

Nikolsburg, July 19th.

The Guard Landwehr Division v. Rosenberg of the I Reserve Corps will arrive by railway at Brünn, with its first echelon this evening. with the others in the next days, and afterwards also half of the Division Bentheim; a part will, perhaps, be able to be sent on by railway as far as Lundenburg. Orders have been given from here that these troops, as fast as they arrive, are to be set in march towards Wilfersdorf, where the Reserve Corps is to join the Elbe Army.

Your Excellency is given this information with the notification that the troops of the I Reserve Corps are to receive their further instructions from Wilfersdorf onwards from the Elbe Army.

No. 194.
To Lieut.-General v. Rosenberg-Gruszczynski, Brünn.
Telegram.

Nikolsburg, July 21st.

The reserve corps is to march in echelons to Nikolsburg, there to close up and await further orders. This is to be communicated to General v. d. Mülbe.

(After the army had approached within two days' march of Vienna, the danger of an attack in superior force from Florisdorf, already considered in the undated draft plan (No. 190), came more and more into the foreground. Accordingly the following orders were issued):—

No. 195.*
To the Commanders of the 1st, 2nd and Elbe Armies.

Nikolsburg, July 19th.

It is His Majesty's intention to concentrate the army in a position behind the Russbach, with the Elbe Army at

---
* See plan 5.

Wolkersdorf, the 1st Army behind Deutsch-Wagram, the 2nd Army as reserve at Schönkirchen. In this position the army is first of all to be able to oppose an attack which the enemy can undertake with perhaps 150,000 men from Florisdorf; secondly, from this position it must either reconnoitre and attack the entrenchments at Florisdorf or be able to march off as quickly as possible to Pressburg, leaving a corps of observation against Vienna. For this purpose the bodies that are already available, *i.e.*, the Elbe Army and then the II Corps, the 6th Division, the Cavalry Corps, and the advance guard of the 1st Army, will move to-morrow, the 20th, first of all only as far as the Weidenbach, between Gaunersdorf and Weikendorf, in order to gain time for the further portions of the army to come up. Both armies will push their advance troops and reconnaissances towards the Russbach in the direction of Wolkersdorf and Deutsch-Wagram. Simultaneously with this advance the attempt is to be made to attack Pressburg by surprise, and to take that place and to secure the possibility of crossing the Danube there. It is left to the Commander of the 1st Army to issue the orders to his forces available for this purpose at Malacka on the left bank of the March. The Commander of the 1st Army will also arrange to bring up again the 5th Division which is still at Holitsch so soon as the conditions there allow.

The 2nd Army has to arrange the continuance of the march for the Guard and VI Army Corps in the direction of Lundenburg or Nikolsburg, as the case may be, and His Majesty counts upon these corps reaching on the 21st inst. the line Drösing—Wilfersdorf for the support, if required, of the 1st and Elbe Armies. How soon the V Army Corps can be brought up the Commander of the 2nd Army will judge and determine by his orders, as it is in all circumstances desirable to appear on the Danube with the greatest possible total strength. Arrangements have been made for bringing up the I Reserve Corps from Prague or from Pardubitz, as the case may be, by railway. The pontoon columns of the 2nd Army which arrive at Köstl to-day are placed at the disposal of the Commander of the 1st Army for effecting the passage of the Danube, for which from the map Theben seems a specially favourable point. The Commander of the 1st Army is requested to attach to the expedition from Malacka to Pressburg the Staff, Artillery and Engineer officers to be charged with the reconnaissance of the place of crossing.

As soon as the restoration of the railway traffic renders it possible a magazine will be formed at Lundenburg in addition to the general reserve magazine for the whole army at Brünn.

Besides this, however, each army must arrange to fill magazines of its own in its own rayon. The present slow advance offers the opportunity of sending stronger requisition parties over a wider extent of country.

The Inspector-General of Artillery (Lt.-Gen. v. Hindersin) has already been requested to form a park of horses and wagons at Auspitz, for the transport of the siege guns expected from home, and the commanders of armies will be good enough to comply with any requests from the Inspector-General for assistance in this matter.

The order already given on the 10th instant for quite summary returns of the strengths of squadrons and batteries has been complied with only by the Elbe Army. These returns are now expected as soon as possible from the other two armies. All three armies must at once report what parties belonging to them have been left behind on the communications, so that an exact account of the actually available battalions, squadrons, &c., can be framed.

No. 196.

To the Commanders of the 1st, 2nd and Elbe Armies.

Nikolsburg, July 20th.

The 1st and Elbe Armies remain to-morrow in their positions on the Weidenbach at Weikendorf and Gaunersdorf. The advance troops pushed forward to the Russbach are to watch any movements of the enemy, and in presence of decided superiority would have to withdraw to the Weidenbach. Should the enemy advance with considerable forces towards the Weidenbach the two named armies will vigorously support one another according to circumstances, and for this purpose must from now keep up continuous communication with one another.

Of the 2nd Army the VI and Guard Corps are to arrive as soon as possible in second line behind the Elbe Army, for which purpose the Guard Corps is to be sent from Lundenburg through Böhmischkrut. The two corps will thereupon spread their billets up to the road from Asparn to Dürnholz, but must also protect themselves on their flank upon the road Vienna—Laa. On the great road from Brünn to Vienna the depôt point Nikolsburg is to be kept free for the I Reserve Corps, which is advancing in small echelons towards the Elbe army; its leading body yesterday reached Brünn and will, presumably, arrive at Nikolsburg to-morrow. The V Army Corps is to join the 2nd Army again from Skalitz by the nearest way through Hohenau; the First Army will have already drawn to itself its 5th Division. At Göding and at Lundenburg the 2nd Army is to leave small parties to protect the magazines there and the railway.

No. 197.
To the Commander of the 1st Army.

Nikolsburg, July 20th.

As His Majesty is to-day prevented from moving his headquarters further to the south His Royal Highness Prince Frederick Charles, in case of an attack by the enemy, will take charge of the action until His Majesty's arrival.

Reports are at once to be sent to Nikolsburg.

(Negotiations had already been in progress for several days at the great headquarters of His Majesty at Nikolsburg with a view to a five days' armistice. The armistice was concluded on July 21st. The troops were informed of the fact by)—

No. 198.
To the Commanders of the 1st, 2nd and Elbe Armies.

Nikolsburg, July 21st.

His Majesty has agreed that during a period of five days, from noon on the 22nd until noon on the 27th, no hostilities of Prussian against Austro-Saxon troops are to take place, and, therefore, from to-morrow morning no movements are to be undertaken which can lead to such hostilities.

A southern line of demarkation will be agreed upon with Austria and will presumably follow the line of the positions at present occupied along the Danube and the Russbach. Details will be communicated to the Commanders of both armies. Staff officers of the 1st and Elbe Armies are to assemble for this purpose at 9 a.m. to-morrow at Wolkersdorf at the quarters of the Quarter-master-General, Major-General v. Podbielski. They must be prepared to give an exact account of the position of the troops, especially of the outposts. The regions within which each of the three armies may be billeted are determined as follows:

The 2nd Army receives the district upon banks of the

March, north of the Zaya, and of the Laksarbrück which flows into the March between Gr. Schützen and St. Johannes. Nikolsburg and the district immediately north of it are to be kept free for the I Reserve Corps, which is arriving there in echelons.

The 1st Army receives a district south of the Zaya and of the Laksarbruck, bounded on the west by the road Vienna—Brünn including the villages situated in it.

The Elbe Army is to have its billets west of this road.

It is desirable and permissible to spread out the billets for the comfort of the troops, but it must be borne in mind that on the expiration of the armistice the whole army should be ready, in case it is ordered, to take a concentrated position behind the Weidenbach.

The Commander of the 2nd Army will be good enough to communicate His Majesty's decision conveyed in the first paragraph above to the I Army Corps, whose Commanding General on his part is to inform the Commandant of Olmütz, with the notification that he too, in case the Commandant agrees, will refrain from hostilities against Olmütz until noon of the 27th instant. Movements of troops and other transports within the regions on this side of the line of demarcation are not affected by the armistice; and therefore, also, any parties in rear which can be spared may be brought up.

Movements of troops into the more extented billets are not to begin until the conclusion of the agreement as to the line of demarcation has been reported by the staff officers on their return from Wolkersdorf.

(In order to make the most of the unoccupied part of Bohemia for supplying the army, and with a view of keeping order in this country, the following orders were issued):—

No. 199.

To the Governor-General of Bohemia, Prague.

Nikolsburg, July 21st.

Mobile columns to be sent out in particular to Pilsen and then to Eger. May use for the purpose and for keeping order the Landwehr battalions garrisoning the railways and the corps of observation forming at Josephstadt and Königgrätz, as well as the mixed brigade of Bentheim's division remaining at Prague.

Is informed that the II Reserve Corps started on the 20th instant to march from Leipzig to Hof.

No. 200.
To the Governor-General of Bohemia, Prague.
Telegram.
Nikolsburg, July 24th.

Circumstances require the immediate military occupation of the districts of Pilsen, Eger and Carlsbad.

All that is left of the I Reserve Corps at Prague is at your disposal. Report how far the troops have advanced into western Bohemia by to-day.

(Copy sent to General v. d. Mülbe, Brünn.)

(To the proposal of the Military Governor of the Kingdom of Saxony, General v. Schack, to make an attempt to take the fortress of Königstein, which was still in possession of the Saxon troops, Moltke replied)—

No. 201.
To General v. Schack, Dresden:
Nikolsburg, July 21st.

Your Excellency has suggested an enterprise against Königstein.

His Majesty does not fail to recognize the desirability of such an action but thinks that considering the peculiar character of the place success cannot be expected with any certainty.

Moreover, the heavy guns at Dresden will probably shortly be needed here. Your Excellency is requested to consider whether General v. Nostitz (Commandant of the fortress of Königstein) might not be informed that all transports past the fortress are being carried on with Saxon matériel and by Saxon subjects and that for every shot fired from the fortress an extra contribution of 10,000 thalers is imposed upon the country.

(For the possibility for a continuation of the war after the expiry of the armistice the following arrangements were made):—

No. 202.
To Major-General v. Blumenthal, Eisgrub.
Nikolsburg, July 22nd.

For the continuance of the operations after the expiry of the five days' suspension of hostilities, it is desirable to appear on the Danube with forces, as far as possible, collected. The

2nd Army for this purpose would have to keep in view especially the following points—

1. The suggestion I have already made in conversation that a division of the I Army Corps should be brought up, if it can be spared, from before Olmütz. In that case it may be assumed that the division can have reached the quarters of the 2nd Army on the Zaya by the 27th instant.

2. We cannot, at this headquarters, gather at what time we may count upon bringing up the 12th Division, which probably practically depends upon the completion of General Lehwald's corps of observation at Königinhof.

3. I do not know the position at this moment of Major-General Knobelsdorff's detachment (one infantry regiment, one cavalry regiment, one battery told off to protect the border of Upper Silesia). According to the last reports it was occupying Austrian Silesia. This occupation, however, seems to have been only temporary, and I note in this connection that the Minister President Count Bismarck lays great stress upon its being renewed, for which purpose, however, a smaller body would suffice.

4. I do not know how far the units of the 2nd Army have received fresh men to fill up their ranks, or when these men are to be expected, or lastly,

5. When the fifteen 4th battalions, destined for the 2nd Army, will arrive.

Your Excellency will inform me as soon as possible with regard to the subjects discussed under 1 to 5, so far as anything has come to your knowledge, so that we here may form a correct judgment concerning the total forces available for the next operations.

No. 203.

To the Commanders of the 1st, 2nd and Elbe Armies, and to the I Reserve Corps, and the 12th Division.

Nickolsburg, July 24th.

Of the I Reserve Corps the Guard-Landwehr Division will distribute itself between Brünn and the Thaya; but in the villages on the great road Brünn—Vienna room is to be left for other troops to march through. The brigade of the Division Bentheim, which has been sent to Pardubitz, will remain in that district until further notice, so that in case of need it can be brought up from Pardubitz to the army by railway.

The 1st, 2nd and Elbe Armies will remain until further orders in the districts indicated for their billets by the order of the 21st instant (No. 198).

No. 204.
To the Commanders of the 1st, 2nd and Elbe Armies.*

Nickolsburg, July 26th.

To-morrow at noon on the expiration of the armistice, the army must have taken up the following position:—

The Elbe Army, on the two roads which it occupies (Ernstbrunn—Vienna and Ladendorf—Vienna) behind the Russbach; the advance troops are then to be pushed out beyond this line. The Elbe Army will also occupy Wolkersdorf with a strong advance guard. The 1st Army will assemble the 5th and 6th Divisions at Bockflüss, with a strong advance guard thrown forward at Deutsch-Wagram, the cavalry corps on the left bank. The 7th Division will move up to the 8th Division at Stampfen, and the II Army Corps will move forward to Marchegg, in order to be ready to act in support either on the right or the left bank of the March. The 2nd Army will stand at the expiry of the armistice with the Guard Corps at Gaunersdorf and the rear portions of the army closed up between the road Brünn—Vienna and the March, as far as the Zaya. The I Army Corps, so far as it is not in front of Olmütz, will continue its march at the discretion of the Commander of the 1st Army, in the first instance on the left bank of the March.

Of the I Reserve Corps the Division Rosenberg on receipt of this order will immediately place itself upon the road Brünn—Laa—Ernstbrunn, and will continue advancing along it until it has reached the rear of the Elbe Army, which the Reserve Corps will then join. The General commanding the Reserve Corps must for this purpose communicate with the Elbe Army and report here the time at which the Division Rosenberg will reach Ernstbrunn.

Those portions of the army which are in rear, for example the 12th Division, the one brigade of the Division Bentheim, &c., will continue their march according to previous orders until further notice, so that they may afterwards eventually be brought up by railway. His Majesty's headquarters go to-morrow to Pirawarth, to which point a battalion of the 2nd Army is to be sent.

* This letter was not sent, because on the same day a formal armistice was concluded for the purpose of the peace negotiations.

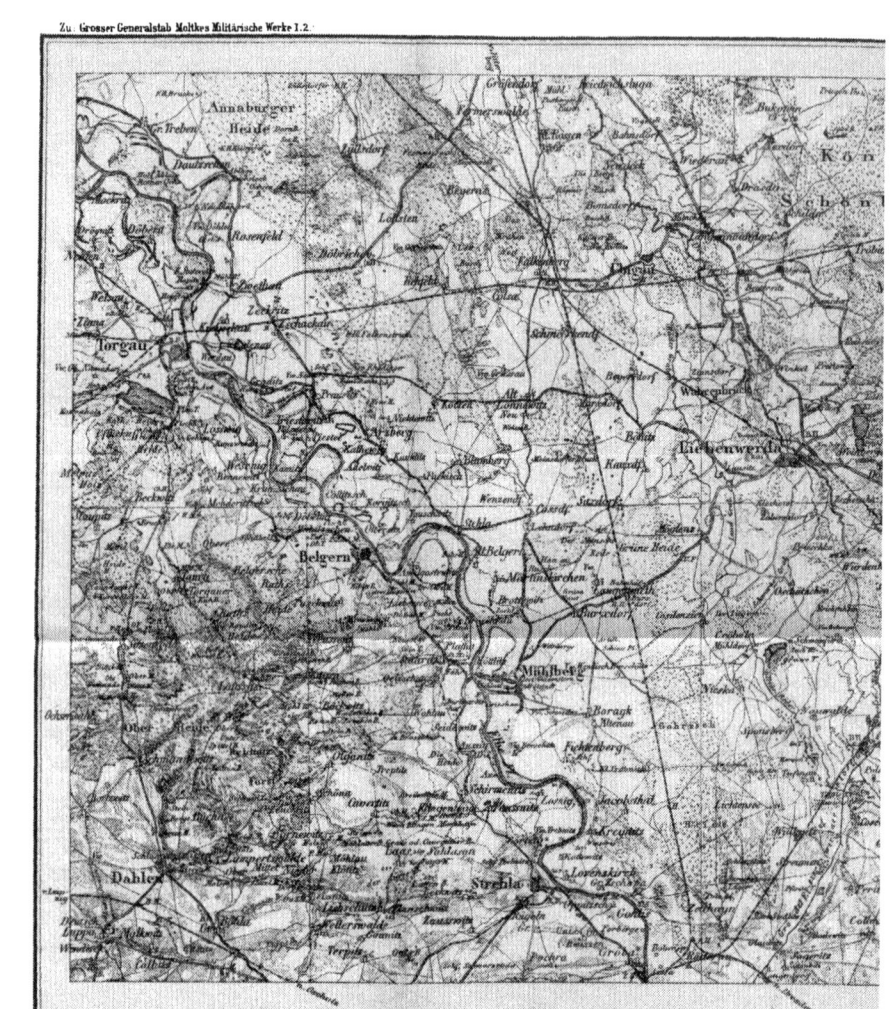

Maßstab 1:200000 der natürl. Länge

Die Höhen sind in Pariser Fuss angegeben. 100 Par: F = 32,48 Mtr.

Bem: Von den Eisenbahnen waren 1866 vorhanden: Die Strecken Jüterbog-Falkenberg-Röderau-Dresden und Röderau-Dahlen-Leipzig.

Plan 2 (zu Nº 57)

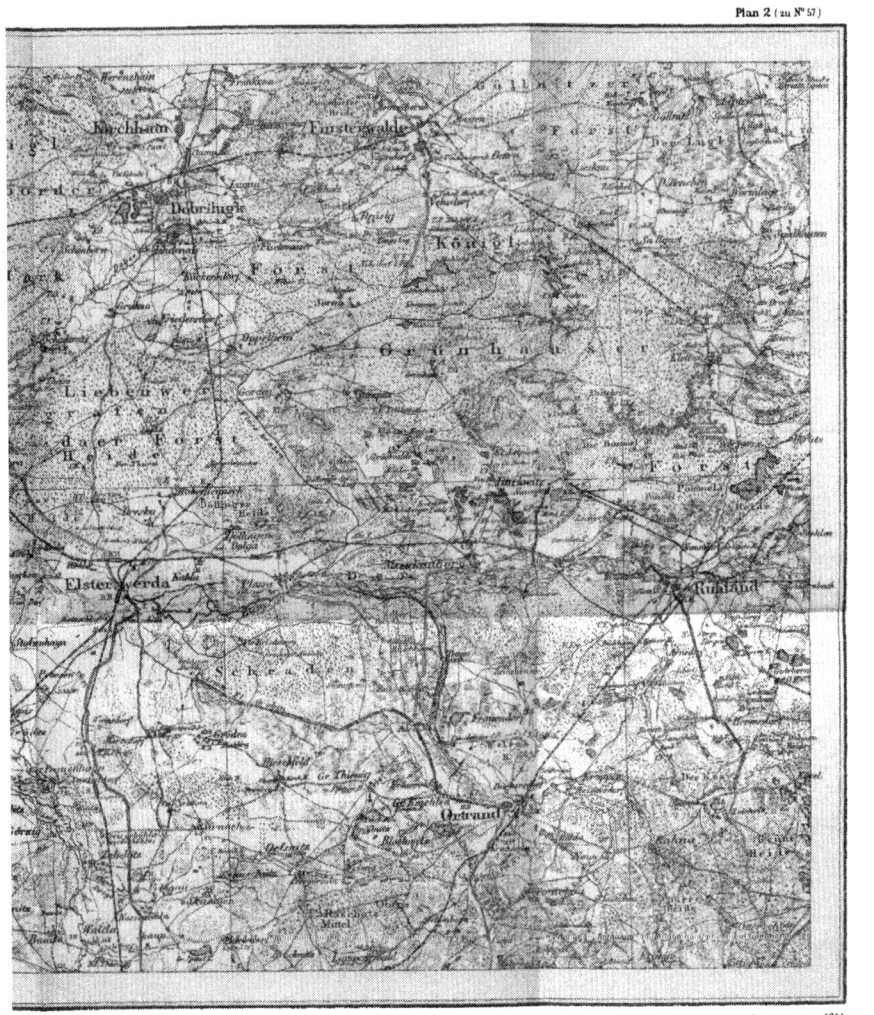

Ordnance Survey Office, Southampton. 1914.

Ausschnitt aus der Sektion (337 Leipzig u. 338
Grossenhayn) der Topographischen
Specialkarte von Mitteleuropa der
Königlichen Preussischen Landesaufnahme

Zu Grosser Generalstab, Moltkes Militärische Werke, I. 2. Plan 3 (zu N° 57.)

Maßstab 1:200 000 der natürl. Länge

Die Höhen sind in Metern angegeben.

Dem Die auf der Karte gezeichneten Eisenbahnen waren 1866 noch nicht vorhanden.

Ordnance Survey Office, Southampton, 1914

Ausschnitt aus der Sektion (308 Luckau) der Topographischen Spezialkarte von Mitteleuropa der Königlichen Preussischen Landesaufnahme.

Zu: **Grosser Generalstab, Moltkes Militärische Werke, I. 2.**

Maßstab 1:200000 der natürl. Länge

0 1 2 3 4 5 6 7 8 9 10 Kilometer

Die Höhen sind in Metern angegeben.

Bem. Von den Eisenbahnen waren 1866 nur vorhanden: Die Strecken Pardubitz -
Königgrätz - Josephstadt - Jaromer - Königinhof und Josephstadt - Skalitz -
Schwadowitz.

Plan 4 (zu N° 151 u. 152.)

Ordnance Survey Office, Southampton. 1914.

Ausschnitt aus der Sektion (126 Königgrätz) der
Topographischen Spezialkarte von Mitteleuropa
der Königlichen Preussischen Landesaufnahme

Zu: Grosser Generalstab, Moltkes Militärische Werke I, 2.

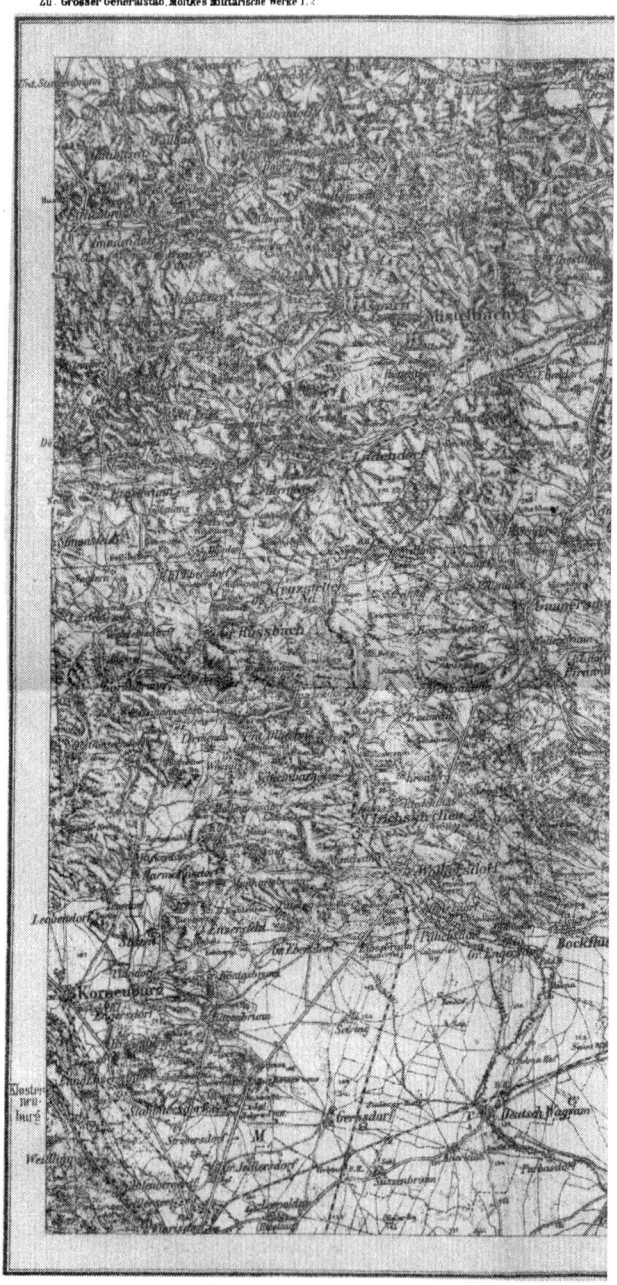

Maßstab 1:200 000 der natürl. Länge

Die Höhen sind in Metern angegeben.

Bem. Von den Eisenbahnen waren 1866 vorhanden: Die Strecken Florisdorf-Korneuburg, Florisdorf-Gänserndorf-Drösing-Lundenburg und Gänserndorf-Pressburg.

Plan 5 (zu N° 195 u 196)

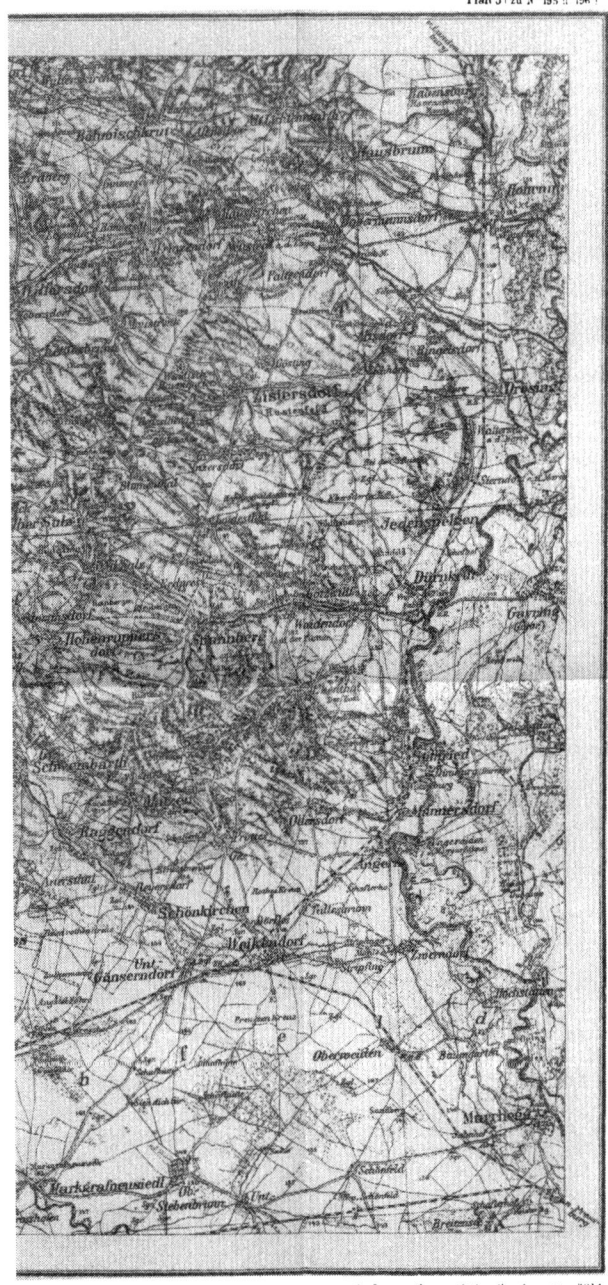

Ordnance Survey Office, Southampton, 1914.

Ausschnitt aus der Sektion (547 Korneuburg) der
Topographischen Specialkarte von Mitteleuropa
der Königlichen Preussischen Landesaufnahme.

www.ingramcontent.com/pod-product-compliance
Ingram Content Group UK Ltd.
Pitfield, Milton Keynes, MK11 3LW, UK
UKHW042006230426
12048UKWH00009B/596